C. S. LEWIS

C. S. Lewis, demobilized and returned to University College, Oxford, 1919. The photograph is by Leo Baker, who returned to Oxford at the same time.

C. S. LEWIS

Memories and Reflections

JOHN LAWLOR

Foreword by Walter Hooper

SPENCE PUBLISHING COMPANY · DALLAS
1998

Published in the United States by
Spence Publishing Company
501 Elm Street, Suite 450
Dallas, Texas 75202

Library of Congress Cataloging-in-Publication Data

Lawlor, John
    C.S. Lewis : memories and reflections / John Lawlor : foreword by
Walter Hooper
        p. cm.
    Includes index.
    ISBN 1-890626-08-2 (hardcover)
    1. Lewis, C. S. (Clive Staples), 1898-1963.   2. Lewis, C. S. (Clive
Staples), 1898-1963—Friends and associates.   3. Fantastic fiction,
English—History and criticism.   4. English teachers—Great Britain—
Biography.   5. Authors, English—20th century—Biography.   6.
Lawlor, John—Friends and associates.   I. Title.
PR6023.E926Z768   1998
823'.912—dc21   98-24265

Printed in the United States of America

For

Kimie Imura

NEW HAVEN FREE PUBLIC LIBRARY
133 ELM STREET
NEW HAVEN, CT 06510

Contents

Illustrations

Foreword

I N HIS INAUGURAL LECTURE as the first Professor of Medieval and Renaissance Literature at Cambridge University, C. S. Lewis urged his listeners to make good use of those brought up in "Old Western Culture" while there were still a few around. "I would give a great deal," he said,

> to hear any ancient Athenian, even a stupid one, talking about Greek tragedy. He would know in his bones so much that we seek in vain. Any moment some chance phrase might, unknown to him, show us where modern scholarship had been on the wrong track for years . . . I stand before you somewhat as that Athenian might stand. I read as a native texts which you must read as foreigners . . . Speaking not only for myself but for all Old Western men whom you may meet, I would say, use your specimens while you can. There are not going to be many more dinosaurs.

Professor Lawlor is one of the few remaining Old Western men. His memories of and reflections on C. S. Lewis are as valuable as they are delightful. It is possible to find out something about Dr. Johnson that Boswell might not have known, but no one—ever—can know the great man as Boswell did. So with Professor Lawlor. Though Old Western culture was widely available when he went up to Magdalen College in 1936, he was tutored by the greatest "Athenian" there, and this book is nearly as valuable as one by Lewis himself.

Old Western culture, with its emphasis on Greek and Latin, is disappearing everywhere, including Oxford. Professor Lawlor is, thus, not only a link between Lewis and the present generation, but a conduit of that culture. This is not to say that what one finds in these rich pages is imitation Lewis. John Lawlor had to qualify for a place at Oxford in order to benefit from Lewis's teaching. Of course, Lewis led his pupil further into English language and literature, and what makes this book so enjoyable is Lawlor's description of what it was like being the "sparring partner" of Lewis for three years. "The disparity between our armament could not have been greater," he says of those tutorials, "his howitzer opposed to my pea-shooter." In time, Professor Lawlor became proficient at the howitzer himself, but we cannot get any closer than these pages to what it was like to be Lewis's pupil.

This wonderful enlargement of our knowledge does not stop there. The range of this book is staggering. John Lawlor was a friend not only of Lewis but all the other Inklings, that remarkable group of friends which included J. R. R. Tolkien, Nevill Coghill, and Hugo Dyson. They emerge from these pages as vividly as Dr. Johnson's friends do from the pages of Boswell. Any ancient Athenian would have been proud to have written this book.

WALTER HOOPER

Preface

T HIS BOOK is an attempt to recollect Lewis "in his habit
as he lived". There are memories of his tutorial work;
of his sallying forth into delighted controversy upon
the name and nature of English studies; his kindness towards
the neophyte researcher; and the solid foundations of a lasting friendship.

To round out the picture, I have drawn upon memories
of such diverse figures as Nevill Coghill and Adam Fox, C. L.
Wrenn and Hugo Dyson, A. L. Rowse and some others, including a close comparison with Tolkien—as postgraduate supervisor and as a towering presence. There is a glance at
undergraduate life in the immediately pre-War years, and, to
complement these sketches, a step-by-step exposition of two
aspects of Lewis's writing—the science fiction and the
Chronicles of Narnia. There is also an assessment of a theme
perhaps too little touched upon in latter-day assessments of
Lewis—his notion of "happiness"—and here I find links with
the Johnson of *Rasselas* and with some of the figures of English nineteenth-century romanticism. Finally, an attempt is

made at determining Lewis's scholarly achievement—always and supremely the exponent of what is to be commended in fellow-writers, whatever the period under review. In a Postscript I offer my best understanding of a complex man, in whom some maddening obstinacies and sword-sharp disclaimers co-existed with an untroubled awareness of the highest order.

The aim has been to produce a book that does not limp along on its footnotes. Such references as are necessary are contained within the text, to invite an uninterrupted reading.

I have drawn on personal correspondence, hitherto unpublished, and on Lewis's annotation of books, once owned by him and subsequently mine. Some parts of this book draw upon "The Tutor and Scholar" (*Light on C. S. Lewis*, ed. Gibb, London 1965) and "*Rasselas*, Romanticism, and the Nature of Happiness" (*Friendship's Garland*, ed. Gabrieli, Rome, 1966), here reprinted with the permission of the respective publishers, HarperCollins Publishers, Ltd., London, and Edizioni di Storia e Letteratura, Rome.

My special thanks go to Joy Mills for an encouraging view of material once discussed at Hawarden; and to Glenys Mothershaw for unremitting care in typing successive drafts.

The book is dedicated to my wife, Kimie Imura Lawlor, who has shared my interest at every turn. In this she has, I believe, come to know Lewis well, as will, we hope, those who care to turn these pages.

JOHN LAWLOR

PART I

MEMORIES

1

The Tutor

"WHAT MOST ELUDES DESCRIPTION is not the excellence of his gifts but the singularity of his essential being." So Housman wrote of his colleague Arthur Platt; and the words are wholly applicable to Lewis. There was, to begin with, the discrepancy between what one expected of the accomplished medieval scholar (and, later, the penetrating exponent of theological and spiritual matters) and the robust, no-nonsense, unmistakably strident man, clumsy in movement and in dress, apparently little sensitive to the feelings of others, determined to cut his way to the heart of any matter with shouts of *distinguo!* before re-shaping it entirely. One quickly felt that for him dialectic supplied the place of conversation. Any general remarks were of an obvious and even platitudinous kind; talk was dead timber until the spark of argument flashed. Then in a trice you were whisked from the particular to fundamental principles; thence (if you wanted) to eternal verities; and Lewis was alert for any riposte you could muster. It was comic as well as breathtaking; and Lewis would see the comedy as readily as the next man. He was, of course, only passing on what he had learned from "the Great Knock". As we may learn from *Surprised by Joy* (1955), the young Lewis was at first as dismayed as any of his own pupils at a conversational technique indistinguishable from viva voce examination. But he learned quickly; and before long the instructor was commending the pupil. In this regard, Lewis never looked back. He was the dialectician all his life; and one must only add that he was superb. Lewis on form (and I do not remember him ever being much below form) was a Black Belt among novices. There was a memorable occasion when in the Hall at Magdalen Dr. Tillyard met him to round off in debate the controversy begun with the publication of Lewis's indictment of "The Personal Heresy". I am afraid there was no debate. Lewis made rings round Tillyard; in, out, up, down, around, back again—like some piratical Plymouth bark against a high-built galleon of Spain. Never was there a more skilful demonstration of "the Great Knock's" skills. As to the issues of the debate, that, perhaps, is another story. There is no doubt that immense dialectical skill can batter an opponent into silence. But, as Adam Fox once reminded us, in the words of Daniel Waterland, "It is one thing to understand the doctrine, and quite another to be masters of the controversy." Lewis's ambition was of course to know the doctrine and to be master of the controversy.

I first met Lewis in October 1936. My notion of Oxford, and Oxford dons, was firmly preconceived: for three years I was to pursue truth in a setting of architectural and spiritual refinement. Dons to me were sports-jacketed figures with pastel ties, reclining under the great chestnut tree at Balliol in apparent indolence, but all the while razor-keen to detect inconsistencies in attitude or standpoint. I say "attitude or standpoint" since formal argument held little appeal. I agreed, of course, that some of the inconsistencies we were after could

be approached ratiocinatively, and examined for logical con-
tradiction; but the deeper kinds of awareness were to be
reached intuitively rather than through rationalisations. This
in fact constituted my justification for studying imaginative
literature at all, rather than history or philosophy or psychol-
ogy. I held that when one sensed (rather than "detected") a
defect of style, a false emphasis of rhythm, or an inadequate
characterisation, one was at that point gaining insight into the
real subject of enquiry, through the gap between the thing made
and its potentiality; and from there one must go forward and
into the work, not outward into analogy and speculation, however brilliant. What I was looking for was not a methodol-
ogy but a way of life, one which would encourage and sustain
a maximum receptivity to works of art. I knew (or thought I
knew) enough about "reality" in the sense of quotidian experience—though there, too, I wanted heightened awareness, not
escape into fantasy or moralised judgement.

Lewis lived in as good a setting as any man for the life of
vigilant aestheticism I had pictured for myself. His rooms were
on the first floor of New Buildings 3, and ran the width of the
building, so that the sitting-room looked out on Magdalen
Grove, the other half of the suite commanding the Cloister,
and, in the background, the incomparable Tower. My first tap
on the door drew a bellowed "Come in!", and there was my
mentor for the next three years—red-faced, bald, dressed in
baggy jacket and flannel trousers (alas! no pastel tie), and
obviously in no mood to waste time—a permanent characteristic, I was to find. For my first Term I read Pass Modera-
tions—bits of Constitutional Law and History, Pliny's *Letters*,
some English literature (Dryden's *Essay of Dramatic Poesy* came
in, I remember), and, as a preparation for an English School
solidly ranged on principles Lewis staunchly upheld, some el-
ementary Anglo-Saxon. The tuition for all except the Anglo-

Saxon would come from others: with Lewis one did the grammar from Sweet's *Primer* and worked up from the early sentences to a piece on King Edmund. I remember only two things about the Anglo-Saxon sessions. One was the suggested translation of *Eala rhu biscop* as "Tut! tut! Your Grace"; the other was my first experience of Lewis's determined impersonality towards all except his very closest friends. I had clean forgotten to come to an extra class which Lewis had generously offered; and I afterwards went to see him with real regret at having been so stupid. He cut short my apologies: "I'm not your schoolmaster, you know." It was coldly said, and coldly meant. If I couldn't keep to the appointed duties of an undergraduate (they were few enough, heaven knows), then doubtless I would sooner or later have to go. But I mustn't think of our relationship as a personal one.

With the Hilary Term we started on the English School proper, and here Lewis was in his element—the more so as, of the choices offered, I had decided to begin with Spenser. The tutorial ritual was always the same. The pupil, gowned and clutching his essay (an affair of some three thousand words or more) sat on the comfortable but shapeless settee. Lewis, smoking vigorously (I never saw him without pipe or cigarettes except when out on a walk) sat in the armchair, pencil in hand; and there he doodled, caricatured, and made an occasional note, while the pupil read aloud (twenty minutes might be an average time). Then Lewis would proceed to an examination of what was said; and often, what was not said. I once reminded him of Ronald Knox's remark: "The prevailing attitude . . . was one of heavy disagreement with a number of things which the reader had not said." The point was taken; the more the pupil showed a capacity for self-defence the better Lewis was pleased. I like to think that he enjoyed some of our tutorials; for the plain fact is that he hated teaching. The reasons for this are not far to seek. In the first place, as a young don (and on into early middle age), Lewis got relatively few pupils in English, and those were of varying quality. In these days of rapid University expansion, with English often leading most others in undergraduate numbers, it requires an effort of imagination to realize how few read the Oxford English School in the between-war years; and, frankly, before the days of "practical criticism" in the schools, how dreadfully amateurish we could be. At Magdalen, one of the larger Oxford Colleges, and one of the few to have a Tutorial Fellow in English, the number of freshmen in 1936 proposing to read English was precisely two: and this is not untypical of the period. In consequence, part of Lewis's tutorial duties was to teach Political Science to Magdalen undergraduates reading History and Modern Greats; and in addition he had a lectureship at University, his old College, which he held until Dyson took it over in, I think, 1946. Secondly, Lewis's own temperament and interests led him very far from any conviction that the study of imaginative literature, even when undertaken by first-rate intelligences, could justify some of the exalted claims made for it. He was correspondingly ready to open the range of the pupil's mind, given fair opportunity. Where he could not strike fire, he tended to accept with ironic resignation; but it did not endear teaching to him. Thirdly—and I have, I believe, kept the true order of importance—Lewis valued time as few men I have met, before or since, have done. After an early breakfast and a walk, nine o'clock in Term time would see him seated at his writing-table, wooden penholder and steel nib moving steadily over the page until the ten o'clock pupil knocked on his door. "The hungry generations tread thee down" was a witticism he ruefully acknowledged. No man was better equipped for silent industry, hour upon hour; and, after the war especially, when undergraduates of all ages flocked into the University, few men had more calls upon their time, not only for tutorial duties but to address the clubs and societies which sprang up on every hand. To Lewis, tutorial work was a school of patience; and if one was ever disappointed that one's best things had gone unregarded, one was also conscious that one's best wasn't good enough to feed and sustain his most remarkable mind.

The effect of this was that a good many of Lewis's pupils, including the very best of them, were reduced to silence, or worse, incoherence when dealing with him. It is one thing to "admit captivity by a higher and nobler mind"; another to find something to say to pass the rest of the hour. Lewis's gifts, then, as a tutor, strike me as representative of both the virtues and the defects of the Oxford tutorial system as it was practised in my time. For some it would prove an unmatched experience in intellectual exhilaration—a sight of wide horizons and a growing sense of "The achievement of, the mastery of the thing". For others, unhappy silence on the part of the pupil, while Lewis would boom away in unavailing efforts to draw a response, or eventually fall silent in turn. Neither category of pupil corresponds neatly with the able and the mediocre-to-weak. Men of high ability would find nothing to say: and men of less ability might cheerfully forge ahead, to make a series of passes which the veteran could joyously beat down, while crying his approval. One thing Lewis never did, in any recollection I have of him: He never imposed his Christianity on the argument. If it was there already (and the great majority of writers we were dealing with were Christian in their cast of mind if not always in any direct allegiance) he would take up the point and develop it. But never would he obtrude his beliefs. Here, as in all other aspects of his life, he was reserved to an almost fantastic degree. The determined and even aggressive joviality was all on the surface: within was a settled contentment, guarded by a schoolboy's contempt for "pi-jaw".

As for me, I passed from dislike and hostility to stubborn affection, and then to gratitude for the weekly bout in which no quarter was asked or given. Lewis's own account, in the preface to *Essays Presented to Charles Williams* (1947), of "the cut and parry of prolonged fierce, masculine argument" perfectly characterises his notion of a good tutorial. It happened that I had ready-made what Lewis as a young don had found necessary to adopt, a position to argue from. His, as he describes it in *Surprised by Joy* was "watered Hegelianism"; mine, hastily acquired in the sixth form and maintained but not adequately scrutinised until the end of my second year at Oxford, was dialectical materialism—"Hegel the right way up". (It showed, by the way, the degree of open-mindedness he practised that he chose me for a Magdalen award, with my clamantly socialist papers before him, when I had thought of myself as God's gift to Lindsay's Balliol, with which Magdalen was teamed for scholarship purposes.) It was the time of the Spanish Civil War, and those on the political Left (though few in Magdalen) were busy organising lunches for refugee funds, collecting money by point-blank asking, and getting up meetings and demonstrations in support of the Spanish Government. I must have been the last man Lewis wanted to see. He valued above all else his privacy, and here was I invading it with requests to give money or to join meetings of the liberally-minded. It must have hurt him very much to refuse money. The scale of his benefactions has become in part known since his death. Lewis was surely one of the most cheerful givers, according to his means, who ever lived. He could not contribute to anything that had an overtly political implication;

but I did get a paper out of him when he inaugurated the English Faculty Society (a venture which came from my and others' dissatisfaction with an English Club that perpetually devoted itself to such notable English writers as Blok, George, Rilke, et al.).

The paper ("Our English Syllabus") expresses perfectly the spirit of Lewis's tutoring: "The student is, or ought to be, a young man who is already beginning to follow learning for its own sake, and who attaches himself to an older student, not precisely to be taught, but to pick up what he can." ("I'm not your schoolmaster, you know.") There were, however, certain things that weren't to be picked up, notably modern literature. Anyone, Lewis declared contemptuously in the same paper, "who wants a tutor's assistance in reading the works of his own contemporaries might as well ask for a nurse's assistance in blowing his own nose". These were, I may add, the days when the farthest reach into modernity dared by the Oxford syllabus was 1830. Lewis had not the least conception of the view best expounded by Eliot, that we need the past in order to understand the present—much less its corollary, that the present, fairly confronted, will enable us to understand the past. He was fond of maintaining that the present was itself "only a period" (a bad one, in his view); but he was not prepared to see the past as only a period. The paper on the Oxford English syllabus should be read along with its companion-piece (both are printed in *Rehabilitations*, 1939), "The Idea of an 'English School'". There, with characteristic humour, Lewis indicates his own conservative position under the appropriate image of trench warfare. "I do not know," he says, "where the last ditch in our educational war may be at the moment; but point it out to me on the trench-map and I will go to it."

Against this redoubtable conservatism I pitted myself in

the weekly tutorial. The disparity between our armament could hardly be greater—his howitzer opposed to my pea-shooter. But to it we went—with increasing goodwill on his side and growing respect on mine. How could a materialist like me have anything on which to base the notion of value? What was the final stage of the supposedly continuous dialectic of history? Could there be an ultimate "synthesis"? Why, if it was inevitable, should we contend for it, much less approve it? The reader may think these were poor English tutorials, perhaps deserving Lewis's own strictures, in *The Abolition of Man* (1943), on "the work of amateur philosophers" when it is substituted for that of "professional grammarians". The reader would be wrong. It was all in the course of business. Week by week I read my essays on Milton, Dryden, Johnson, whatever—and week by week we joined battle—sometimes an indolent grenade or two, sometimes all-out offensive. I was allowed the initiative on every occasion; Lewis gave me the choice of ground and of weapons and of course beat me every time. But towards the end of the second year, when we had moved into later medieval literature, I found him less dismissive. On my side, philosophically, I was moving towards a kind of socialism which could be described as enlightened self-interest with a strong bias towards left-of-centre political action. *Language, Truth, and Logic* had appeared, and it left no room for either his idealism or my own thorough-going materialism. By the middle of my third year I do believe I was interesting him. I remember, in particular, his approval of my maintaining the non-realistic nature of a large part of Shakespearian characterisation. Like any good tutor he showed me how the case I had sketched could be made stronger, introducing me to an area of criticism which, while it gave comforting support to my argument, seemed to him largely misconceived. By the end of my time as his pupil, I won't say that the cycle of Old Knock and young Lewis had wholly repeated itself. There was still far too much in my position that he thought mistaken, and certainly I had made too little advance in dialectics. But the day did come, many years later, when Lewis cried halt. "You're too quick for me," he said, one golden morning in a Headington pub garden. One more instance of his generosity.

Those who did not know Lewis as a tutor may catch a glimpse in his own Dr. Dimble (*That Hideous Strength*, 1945), interrupted in a matter of real importance by "my dullest pupil, just ringing the bell . . . I must go to the study and listen to an essay on Swift beginning 'Swift was born'. Must try to keep my mind on it, too, which won't be easy." There is all of Lewis in that, not forgetting the willed attention to the mediocre performer. For anyone who thought, however hazily, that the study of English literature was to consist in conscientious excerpting from standard authors while juggling accepted phrases of approbation, he was a shock and a tonic. Nevill Coghill, among the earliest of his post-War friends, found the exactly right word—Lewis was "formidable". Yet he was not out to shock—least of all by denigrating his authors. It was for this reason, indeed, that he viewed supervision at Cambridge, in some of its more renowned practitioners, with considerable reserve. The Oxford tutor, I seem to remember him saying, on first encounter with his pupil, asks, "What have you been reading?"; and he follows on from there, taking the book and showing its virtues as well as its limitations, to lead in open-minded enquiry to those who have been called major writers. The virtues, be it noted: Lewis had no use for mere "debunking", least of all when it started with an unargued superiority of "modern" (in no strictly examined sense) against

"ancient" or (worse) "medieval". But the Cambridge supervisor, he said, was likely to receive the answer to the same first
question ("What have you been reading?") with the menac-
ing words, "Oh, you've been reading *that* have you . . ." and
then proceed to the knife-work of murdering to dissect, in
order to sweep the vile body aside to make room for the cer-
tified masterpieces. There was generosity in Lewis's protest:
he saw no justification for vilifying the dead. When he
characterised, in his *Experiment in Criticism* (1961), the kind
of critic for whom the great names of the past "are as so many
lamp-posts for a dog", he really did mean "lamp-post", a light
shining out over the dwelling places of civilized man.

I could as readily as anyone deplore the influence of "the
Great Knock": his meeting with Lewis was perhaps one of the
least fortunate in intellectual history. The shy boy from Belfast,
making his naïve comments on the Surrey countryside, became the one who had no small talk; who talked habitually,
as Johnson did, for victory. But never was there a more mag-
nanimous victor. At times he could give the impression of
conceit ("I am as conceited as the next man," he cheerfully
wrote), or even arrogance. But he had few illusions about himself, and none about his standing. He wrote to me, not long
after inaugurating the Medieval and Renaissance Professorship, "my medieval mission at Cambridge is, so far, a *flop
d'estime*". Self-conscious, yes: but self-deluded, never. I count
it the greatest good fortune to have sorted out my intellectual
equipment, once a week in Term-time for three years under
his vigilant and genial eye.

Oxford in those years immediately preceding the Second
World War must, at this distance, seem remote indeed. Perhaps something can be done in the next chapter to tighten the
focus.

2

Magdalen, 1936–1939

MAGDALEN IN 1936 was widely known as the College attended by the Prince who was soon to succeed to the Throne. There was a dinner during my first Term in which undergraduates and dons, dinner-jacketed to a man, met to celebrate the forthcoming Coronation. "How nice to see so many well-dressed men in this Hall", said President George Gordon amusedly, rising to toast the future King. All was changed, of course, very soon; but it was a moment to remember.

I found that my Marxist views were shared by one other member of the College, Robert Conquest, nowadays the shrewdest critic among Sovietologists but then a wholehearted believer. Together we founded Magdalen's first left-wing society, named after Ralph Fox (not to be confused with Adam Fox, of whom more later), and we were busy in collecting money for the Government side in the Spanish Civil War, taking part in demonstrations and meetings at every opportunity, and seeking out the like-minded in other Colleges. The most prominent of these was Philip Toynbee, and I bore an introduction to him. Toynbee listened with grave courtesy to the account of Conquest's and my doings; assured me he was always there at need; and vanished from my ken. He was, it will be understood, a whole year senior to me; and his time was, as befitted an attractively *louche* leader, much taken up. Bob and I had an ally (not very political, but determined not to let the Establishment have things all its own way) in John Blakeway, who could be relied upon to add his voice at need.

One memory will serve for many. Duff Cooper, War Minister in Chamberlain's "National" Government, turned up to speak to the University's Conservatives assembled in the Hall at Magdalen. Entrance to the meeting was of course barred for us. We hit upon the stratagem of marching through the Cloister shouting this rallying cry:

> *Down with the National Government,*
> *The Government of hunger and war;*
> *And up with the third Labour Government*
> *(But not like the sods we had before).*

Beside the faithful John Blakeway we had one other ally—a Welshman, conveniently lodged in the Chaplain's Quad, who serenaded the adjacent Hall windows to the tune of "Colonel Bogey" played fortissimo upon the trumpet. The meeting proceeded unhurriedly to its conclusion; but we felt that one small voice of protest might have been heard.

A kindly eye was kept on undergraduates in general by Adam Fox, Dean of Divinity. Open house was held at 10:00 PM—"beer, tea or coffee". He was, of course, a devoted friend of Lewis and the story of his election as Lewis's candidate for the Professorship of Poetry has often been told. I add the tiny detail that, calling on the evening of the election, I found pinned to Lewis's closed door a foolscap sheet exhibiting a Fox crowned with laurels, with, receding into the margins, on the one side a visibly Stricken Deer (the legend KEKIL made all plain) and, on the other an indeterminate figure similarly routed. Lewis's freehand drawing must have beguiled many a tedious tutorial hour. I wish I had been bold enough to seize this happily triumphant proclamation.

Unfailingly hospitable Adam Fox was; and in later years I often visited him in his snug dwelling adjoining Westminster Abbey, where his twin sister Eve kept house for him. It is pleasant to recall a Dean of Divinity (as Magdalen terms its principal Chaplain) who in impeccable couplets gave instructions for the conduct of his own funeral, including the admonition:

> But listen, Chaplain! Oh whate'er you do
> Keep to the mind of Sixteen Sixty-Two.
> Let no false note from Nineteen Twenty-Eight
> Intrude upon my obsequies, for such I hate.

As to his Magdalen abode, there was one curious circumstance. Adam dwelt at the top of St. Swithun's Staircase 1. As with all College staircases, the names of the inhabitants were displayed at ground level; and at the foot of Swithun's Staircase 1 the list terminated in fitly descending order from "Rev. Adam Fox" to "Joseph". Adam told me with quiet glee that one day, visited by an aunt or two (he appeared to have an ample supply) and announcing his intention to make tea, one lady expressed polite surprise—could not his page do it for him? His page? Yes, Joseph (such a sweet name), nestling at the stair's foot ready to leap to his master's bidding.

"Joseph" was in fact Keith Joseph, later to become Mrs. Thatcher's pre-eminent guru and to take his place in the House of Lords. I remember him well, for he took it upon himself to advance the cause of General Franco against the Republi-

can Spanish Government. Two Spanish officers visited Magdalen under Keith's tutelage and there was a general invitation to meet them. Hot for controversy I came along to point out that their opposition to the democratically elected government was hardly a "national" movement, drawing as it did on Moorish levies. But Keith bore no ill-will. He was always an intent listener; and though we met seldom in later life I found him sympathetic and just (though not, whatever the topic, noticeably disposed to alter his view). Certainly, he played with characteristic skill (for the Magdalen College Dramatic Society) not only the page in Maurice Baring's *Catherine Parr* but the more testing roles of a burgher of Lichfield and Stephen Giraud, valet to Michael Denison's Lord of Thornton, in Thomas Egerton Wilks's *The Maniac Lover*. Clearly, a man of parts.

Oxford, then, in the years immediately preceding the Second War, was a lively enough place politically. It was no doubt the thought that I had been lurking in some Marxist coven that prompted the curt dismissal, "I'm not your schoolmaster"—which lodged itself, long afterwards, in the dialogue of a play where a kindly Tolkien was shown as reproving Lewis for this perhaps high-handed stance. But Lewis bore no malice and on a later occasion cheerfully responded to an invitation to address that public meeting which would (we hoped) expose the Honour School of English in all its antiquated ways to appropriate ridicule. I say "well", for it was part of the left-wing aim of those days to infiltrate (blessed word, with all its overtones of purposeful intrigue cum high-minded crusade) the "student body", and in this endeavour I had an ally from another College. Lewis, of course, sensed that we hoped for a demolition job. But, agreeing to give the talk, he pointed out that our name for the newly-formed association, the English Faculty Society, to be floated for general recruitment at this first talk, was plainly misconceived. "Faculty" in Oxford usage could only mean the body of appointed University Teachers. But a solution was ready to hand. Let us think of the proposed new association, Lewis suggested, as the English Difficulty Society; and all went forward swimmingly. The paper Lewis gave is of course the one reprinted in *Rehabilitations* ("Our English Syllabus"), and I am bound to say the revolutionary cause went no further along its planned course.

I count my second and third years as the best of my tutorial time. The attractions of Marxism had faded. Since either the war or the revolution would come before Final Examinations I might as well spend my time finding out rather more about English Literature, if only for the growing fun of meeting my tutor better equipped for the weekly adversarial bout. The guess at how long was left wasn't so far out. My last year opened with the Munich fiasco; and it closed (in June 1939) with Oxford's air-raid sirens sounding their wailing rehearsal for September's declaration of war.

In my last undergraduate year (1938-39) I had come to know Nevill Coghill. He and Lewis had combined to run an unofficial class for a selected group of finalists drawn from different Colleges—an "intellectual aristocracy", as Lewis beguilingly put it. The plan was to meet weekly and discuss an essay prepared in turn by each member. I remember a simply stunning performance by Herbert Howarth—on the then unpromising topic of Pope. Discussion, each time, was uninhibited, with Lewis well to the fore in prompting any laggards. I think of those meetings, originating as they did in the benefit Coghill and Lewis had themselves received in George Gordon's time, as a forerunner of the Inklings, the later Thursday evening sessions in Magdalen.

Coghill, of course, was far from being, or wanting to be, any sort of dialectician. His consuming passion was the theatre, and it is fully reflected in the book Auden and I offered as an appropriate *Festschrift*, *To Nevill Coghill from Friends* (1966). But I would like to enter a word of special admiration for Coghill the letter-writer. Endlessly fertile, unfailingly receptive of suggestion or difference, prompt in the highest degree (a reply by return of post was his ordinary practice), and all in a wonderfully fluent script. To have such a correspondent was itself an enlargement of life. I remember, as a very young don, that, having dared to write dismissively of some of his renderings of *Piers Plowman*, I thought I should first go and see him, to read out what I was to publish. He took it in good part. We looked at the text and agreed to differ: and it made no change whatever to a friendship alive and vibrant to the day of his death.

After he and his brother Paddy (Sir Jocelyn) had moved to Lydney in "mild Gloucestershire", I came bearing some small mementos of the battle of Isandlhwana. Nevill, it may be recalled, had been named for that forbear who, dying in the attempt to save the Regimental Colour, had been awarded the British Army's first posthumous VC. Receiving the shards I had collected on a visit to the battlefield, Paddy's gratitude knew no bounds. When I came to leave nothing would do but he must drive me along the pathways of the Forest of Dean— much to the barely concealed alarm of Nevill and the household, for Paddy was one of those drivers of an earlier tradition whose guiding principle was to show no hesitation or doubt at any turn of the road which might occasion caution in lesser men. It is of course a style which has its proud origin in cross-country riding. The car must never feel any doubt in the capability of the driver. The three of us once drove, Paddy at the wheel, some way into Hampshire, to see a memorial effigy which Nevill believed to be that of Chaucer's wife. We all returned safely: and speaking for myself, I can guarantee that no fear was shown, whatever the inward terror. All in all, Nevill Coghill remains an incomparable man. Lewis's first impression of him was absolutely right. A man you could imagine fighting a duel: yes, and one who would be simply unaware of any trick, yours or his, that might give an unfair advantage.

I must not fail to say something of W. H. Lewis—Warnie. Lewis's eleven o'clock tutorial pupil was the fortunate recipient of a cup of tea (a large one, of course). Then Warnie would retreat to the little inner study and resume the steady tap-tap on the ancient machine. His was a self-possessed routine; a retired military man who occupied himself with the task of setting in order the Lewis family papers. No one, as far as my experience goes, could ever guess at the alcoholism which became generally known after his death. Warnie had a schoolboy's sense of fun when dealing with Jack Lewis's friends—"ragging" would be the appropriate word. Owen Barfield, in particular, he would tease as arch-exponent of the wider oneness of the greater whatever-it-is. I treasure a letter written in response to a postcard sent from the United States—from as sober (and not noticeably excessively high-spirited) a trio as would include Clyde Kilby and Barfield:

> 51, Ringwood Road,
> Risinghurst Estate,
> Headington Quarry,
> Oxford
>
> 4th May 1966.

To Messrs. Kilby, Barfield, and Lawlor Ltd. (Pardon, it should of course have been *Inc.*)

From the handwriting on the card and the flippant nature of its content I gather that in Salem, Mass. the pubs are open on Saturday afternoons? Please don't send Kilby over here on a stretcher; I want to have a talk with him, not to listen to his incoherent maunderings in the local hospital.

I'm ashamed to say I've never read Hawthorne, but I like the look of his house.

Is he any good? Personally I'm battling my way through Mr. Homer, His Iliad.

Of course I don't know what it is like in the original Greek, but in translation I'm finding it rather dull and very perplexing—except the similes and the all too rare glimpses of domestic life which are both excellent. Did all these damned ancients have two or three aliases? Interesting to note that the main tactical objective of a battle in those days was to steal as much armour as you could from the dead.

Jack's *letters* came out on 22nd April—or rather the book which Jock Gibb's tame editor made out of *my* book; but it's not bad all the same. I see you've managed to gatecrash into it. I purposely refrained from asking you to send me contributions as I had my sights trained on a public which didn't want to hear about the Utterness of the Nothingness and topics of that sort! (This remark is addressed to Barfield.)

Much talk about the Budget here today, but having ascertained that there is no increase in Income Tax, liquor, or tobacco, I've dismissed the subject from my mind and wish other people would not talk to me about it.

I'm off next week to a borrowed house in Suffolk for a fortnight—complete with housekeeper, car, and chauffeur.

When are you dissolute trio due to reach England?
With salaams to all three of you,

Yours ever,
Warnie.

It will be noticed that he had moved from The Kilns. Later,
moving back, he wrote with practical counsel on my interest
in a neighbouring house and welcomed the possibility that we
might meet more often. Completing his own move, he wrote
triumphantly, "Believe it or not, there were *no* breakages, and
none of my books are missing!" He stuck resolutely to his self-
appointed tasks, though without much confidence in the out-
come. But a cheerful insouciance always broke through, as
in this letter of 31 January 1966:

> Many thanks for your kind and encouraging note of the
> 27th. When one is old, tired, and not too well a letter
> like yours acts as a tonic. I shall keep it by me for the
> moment when I get my proofs—always the nadir of the
> writer's life; one plods along saying at intervals "God, what
> tripe; is there anyone outside a lunatic asylum who would
> give six pence for a copy of it".

One figure from my early days deserves mention for his
relation to C. S. Lewis. A. L. Rowse, whose brisk acerbity is
perhaps better known than his true kindness of heart, had early
on invited me, the merest undergraduate arrival in Oxford, to
lunch at All Souls. I thought it might make an agreeable return to have him to lunch in Magdalen with Lewis, and Jack
Gray (later historian at Queen's, Belfast) to make up a four-
some. After the briefest of desultory talk over sherry, Rowse
persistently shot teasing one-liners to Lewis. At first, he was
gruffly shaken off: but, persisting, Rowse received the most

gruelling of dismissive cross-examinations. Leslie the intuitive Celt was ground to dust by Battling Jack, Police-Court
solicitor unrivalled in dialectic and the crushing put-down.
Reduced in the end to silence, Rowse stayed behind as the
others left. No sooner had the door closed behind them than
he swivelled round to declare, unsubdued, "I never knew Lewis
was such a fool, such a fool".

I am reminded of the dictum that in every fat man there
is a thin one longing to get out. Rowse, I know, will forgive
me for claiming that under the rebarbative figure he shows to
the world lies an intuitive and immediate response to the
young, and an instant and withering scorn for mere dialectic.* Lewis, of course, had the first of these qualities, but not
the faintest insight into the second. If you were not worth his
cross-examination he could have no more to say. And in this
respect there could never be any real change.

---

* Since these words were written, A. L. Rowse has died (3 October 1997).

3

Oxford, 1946 and After

RETURNING TO OXFORD after six years in the Army, I once again climbed the stairs of Staircase 3, New Buildings. Lewis was trundling a fire-screen into position. "Sorry I can't stop: I'm entertaining—at least I *hope* I'm entertaining—some friends." Of course: it was Thursday evening, and what I later came to know as the Inklings were assembling. Same old baggy jacket and trousers, same old inflexible sense of time. I use "inflexible" advisedly. Many years later, invited to dine with him at Magdalene, Cambridge, I had proposed a slight change in arrangements. "Oh, you last-minute people!", he cheerfully grumbled. I have often wanted to be one of those who can unaffectedly fleet the time carelessly, as they did in the Golden World; but I am as little capable of being one of the last-minute people as any man I know. I give this detail for its reflection of Lewis's sense that an inevitably timed succession, not to be departed from, was inseparable from any true conception of duty—an unsleeping moralist's awareness of the real frame-work in which choice is to be exercised. He approved Jeremy Taylor's exact divisions of guidance to Christian living: "The Right Use of Time"; "The Choice of Friends"; and so on. A cage of constraint, no doubt. But he was happy in it, and it will be remembered that when an American interviewer ventured sympathy for a somewhat monotonous existence he replied, unaffectedly, "I *like* monotony".

On my return to Magdalen I was under Lewis's initial direction. The idea was to read for a B.Litt. degree. Neither he nor I had any illusion as to the worth of a B.Litt. in itself. It was to be simply an opportunity for a young scholar to read himself into a wider range than had been covered in the three years of undergraduate work: and this, of course, was all the more necessary for me after six years of enforced illiteracy. Lewis quoted with approval Gilbert Ryle's dictum: "In my day we had literacy and illiteracy. Now there's B.Litteracy." So the B.Litt. it was to be, and I returned to school with the Preliminary course. There, in Magdalen, I enjoyed the palaeography class run by Neil Ker, whose unfeigned joy in this kind of detective work was immediately infectious. One other Magdalen savant, R. W. Chapman, suavely communicated what might be found in the Bodleian. His polite diffidence was a reminder of the astonishment George Gordon, President of Magdalen, had felt when, on first coming to Oxford from Glasgow, he encountered the mannered indifference of an Oxford audience. It is to be remembered that Lewis once said good-humouredly of Gordon (in his Oxford eminence), "You felt that for him literature was a demn'd obleeging business". It wasn't deserved: but it is a reminder that the least hint of a genteel tradition would bring Lewis instantly on guard.

Across the road in Merton was another Scot who had never, in any sense, succumbed to Oxford. David Nichol Smith, who had succeeded Gordon in the Merton Chair of English Literature, instructed the B.Litt. candidates in the history of

English literary scholarship. Fifteen or so of us sat around the long table, Americans, enviably profiting from the G.I. Bill of Rights, well to the fore, and there Nichol Smith regularly brought from his collection in 20 Merton Street editions of the authors on whom he discoursed. I mention it for the impulse it could give to buy while buying was still within even our limited range. Long before, Lewis had asserted "You'll never be much good unless you go without dinners to buy books". It was not until much later that he disclosed that this was a piece of advice that he had received from his own tutor, and he thought it worth passing on (without, he explained, necessarily following it himself). This love of comic absurdity, disarmingly jovial, was one of the characteristics that have puzzled some admirers. The only response to a Northern Irish "wheeze" is respectful silence—until, it may be, your turn should come.

So much for my attendance at the Prelim. classes. Lewis had still to help me find a topic for the intended thesis. When I say "help" the reader may picture a benevolent mentor ransacking the store-house of English studies for promising lines his pupil might follow. No such thing. "Can't pour water into a sieve", he snorted. But he had made one suggestion which, though no use for the immediate purpose, remained with me. Why not something on Malory? I jumped at the chance, bought Vinaver's 1929 monograph, and set about finding a theme. All to no avail. "That bloody Frenchman", he growled at our next meeting, "Sitting on the Winchester manuscript. Nobody can do anything until after he publishes, and that'll be too late for you." So it was to be farewell to anything of consequence on Malory. It will be known that it was Lewis who, when Vinaver's *Works of Sir Thomas Malory* at last appeared, wrote the *Times Literary Supplement* review (June 1947), anonymously, as was the custom in those days. There was a minor consequence, which offers a sidelight on his friendship, still strong at this time, with Tolkien. Lewis had already bought Vinaver's three volumes when they first appeared. He sold the review copies to Tolkien. I linger on "sold" for, though Lewis was the most generous of benefactors with the income from his religious writings, he was almost comically simple in any matter he took to require exact calculation. I once drove him from Cambridge to Oxford (never an easy journey by public transport). When it came to paying the bill for our lunch *en route*, where almost anyone else would have proposed to pay for both, Lewis insisted on a laborious calculation of how much he as my passenger owed me for petrol and then subtracted this dubious sum from his half of the bill, looking to me to pay the remainder. There is something very innocent in this— an Ulsterman's determination to get every jot and tittle right, more especially in matters of no real concern. The spirit of his father's habitual (and often irrational) concern with petty expenditure—the P'daytabird at his worst—had been unconsciously absorbed. I once came upon some notes Lewis had made, preparing for a College meeting, and was struck by an endearingly clumsy simplicity. Truly, he was never a man for business in even the simplest sense that includes good manners. Readers of *The Pilgrim's Regress* (1933) will recall that the Pilgrim John was no match for Mr. Worldly Wise—his "social experience" not being "extensive". Certainly, Lewis's behaviour could be disconcertingly awkward and abrupt. Emerging from a Senior Common Room where, an honoured guest, he had been entertained to the full rituals of port, brandy, and cigars, and meeting his brother, silent in the street by St. Mary's, he eagerly burst out, "I've just been at dinner where they pass the evening newspapers with the port!" His host, accompanying him so far, silently took his leave. I remember him, red-faced and stout, giving poor Joy his arm, with a quart flagon, awaiting refill, thrust under the other elbow. Nothing could more vividly recall Johnson and his dear Tetty: Clumsiness and stridency were inseparable. Maurice Platnauer, kindest of all men, was once asked by a visitor to Oxford, anxious not to miss sight of the great man, what C. S. Lewis looked like. "Like a country gentleman", responded Maurice; and then, thoughtfully, "Well, country, anyway".

But I have come to praise Lewis. These are all traits of a man whose company was a treasure indeed; whose assertions dogmatic, clamant, knock-down, took your breath away. I am sometimes reminded of that Subaltern in *Surprised by Joy* (1955) who, bereft of all power of argument, could only cry, "Uncle Ben'd talk to you. He'd tell you". Lewis was Uncle Ben alright, born to put down all opposition. He reminded Austin Farrer, recalling the pitched battles of earlier Socratic Club meetings, of the impatient Warhorse, "snuffing the imminent battle and saying 'Aha!' at the sound of the trumpet". Everything could be war: and in that war no quarter was asked or given. Behind it all lay Lewis's determined privacy, the central citadel of his being.

Owen Barfield, with whom (of course) Lewis had his "Great War", observes acutely the remarkable combination in Lewis of intellectual maturity, "laced with moral energy", and "a certain psychic or spiritual immaturity". I return to this when looking into Lewis's fictional writing. But the sheer *noise* he could make in swift rejoinder, undoubtedly unnerving, was no affectation but genuinely spontaneous, *une condition d'être*. There must be war, for, as he proclaimed from the masthead of his best book, "Opposition is True Friendship". It was instinctive with him that no-one deserved real interest who was not worth challenge; and this was certainly a kind of compliment. But the illusion that war was a necessary condition of friendship was twin to the illusion that friendships were of necessity permanent, unaltering. It is to a friendship that underwent change that I now turn, and to a friend who was above all offended by sheer noise, the trumpet ever sounding to battle.

I begin with outward appearance, and at once there is striking contrast. Tolkien was unmistakably good-looking— a well-shaped head, delicate hands and feet, and, rarity among donnish heads, well-combed hair. His clothes were neat, his movements calm and controlled. One characteristic of Tolkien made it decidedly hard to follow his utterance—certainly in lectures, and often in conversation. He originally had two prominent front teeth which overlaid the lower lip; and when you add to this a pipe-stem rigidly locked in place you have difficulties that were pretty well insuperable. Lewis and Tolkien were of course inveterate smokers, Lewis at the famed sixty cigarettes a day rate, Tolkien invariably the pipe man. But they exemplified very different styles of lecturing. Lewis at full voice and unashamedly near-dictation speed regularly drew and rewarded full audiences in the Big School on the upper floor. Tolkien, on the ground floor and in much smaller compass, could be consistently heard only by those who squeezed into the front row. Once again we catch a glimpse of a polite tradition, exasperating in even its best exponents. In Oxford, as it then was and had long been, it was not to be supposed that the speaker should be aware of anything so catchpenny as an *audience*.

I cannot refrain from sketching the potential embarrassment even the most attentive listener could be caused by a tradition of laconic inaudibility. Summoned to dinner by Lord

David Cecil a young colleague of mine was asked, after dessert, whether he cared for the barley. Rapidly decoding this, he understood he was being invited to express any liking for whisky. Politely he responded that Yes, he did: distinctly so. Preferably neat, though water might come into it. Decidedly not ice, though. He felt that something was amiss, and soon there were signs that the evening was at an end. It was some time towards afternoon on the following day that he realised that his views had been sought on the ballet. Those who would wish to study the matter can confidently be referred to any of Lord David's pupils from the days of his tutorial Fellowship at New College. More accessible is the tantalisingly brief transcript we owe to Kingsley Amis—or, to be exact, John Wain, in Kingsley Amis's *Memoirs* (1991): "dough mean . . . looks like Chauthah . . . dough mean . . . looks like Dvyden . . ." True, all true.

It was to Tolkien that I was now to go. A subject for my proposed B.Litt. thesis had been found. Lewis had been reading the *Revelations* of Julian of Norwich, at that time available, he thought, only in the modernisation by Grace Warrack. Would I like to try my hand at an edition? If so, a supervisor (in the Oxford sense, one who looks after the intending author of a postgraduate thesis) had to be appointed. It happened that in the far-off days of my last Term as an undergraduate I had discussed with Lewis the possibility of work after the first degree. Intriguingly, there was a Diploma in Philology, and Lewis had at once telephoned Tolkien on the matter. Everything, of course, was cancelled by the outbreak of war: but in early 1946 Tolkien, who was designate Merton Professor (on vacating the Anglo-Saxon Chair) took me on to read for a thesis proposing an edition of Julian of Norwich.

My first and abiding impression was one of immediate

kindness. Tutored by Lewis I had expected to be tested with a few falls, so to speak. But the gentle creature who sucked his pipe and gazed meditatively along its stem seemed interested only in what he could do to help. Help, certainly, was needed. I should explain that the English School of those days was divided into three Courses—the first of which was determinedly philological; the second, I understood, preponderantly philological, a sort of half-way house if that can be envisaged when it is borne in mind that the third Course (the one I had taken) though mainly "literary" included three "language" papers—Old English, Middle English, and a particularly tricky History of the English Language. Naturally, those who aspired to a B.Litt. in a "medieval" topic (Julian wrote in the 14th century) ordinarily came from the ranks of Courses One and Two. I was very much aware of this. But under Lewis's energetic guidance I had read the early authors with no less delight than the later ones, and I thought it no real hindrance to move either side of the line "medieval"/"modern". Let me add, to prevent any misunderstanding of the word "modern", that in 1946 Oxford's farthest reach into modernity was the year 1830. As a young don I was dutifully to attend Faculty meetings at which it was regularly resolved that "the 19th Century be introduced" (that has a pleasing air of *gentillesse*)— but always with the Augustinian reservation, Not yet. So to Tolkien I went, resolved to do my best as an intending medievalist but acutely aware of my shortcomings as a proper "language" man.

Tolkien was moving into a College room at Merton, and was exhilarated at the prospect. He had spent many years at Pembroke College as Professor of Anglo-Saxon. But he had made very little claim on the College and, truth to tell, thought less than highly of it and its senior members. The point is well illustrated by his attitude towards his successor in the Anglo-Saxon Chair, C. L. Wrenn. Wrenn had been a University Lecturer before the war, when he toiled unceasingly as a tutor to those many undergraduates who came from Colleges where some tuition might be provided in matters literary, none in "language"—i.e., Old English, Middle English, and the dreaded A4, History of the English Language. There were, of course, shifts and stratagems. In my first year I had been instructed in Anglo-Saxon by Lewis—for the first two Terms in Sweet's *Primer* and, later, some *Beowulf* which Lewis encouraged his pupils to read aloud. I recall with delight some rousing declamatory feats, with Lewis taking his turn in fine style. With Wrenn one went decorously to his house in North Oxford, at an evening hour. Wrenn was truly indefatigable. He spent long hours at this tutorial work, undertook external University examining wherever he could find it, marked school examination scripts—and all under the handicap of partial sight, reading through a hand magnifier and speaking habitually with eyes half-closed—which did nothing to reassure his interlocutors.

Tolkien's attitude towards all this was a mixture of admiration and jocular scorn. In earlier days the two men had been good, though perhaps not close, friends. There is an anecdote of the two walking home, fur-hatted in the snow, from a North Oxford party, and claiming to be two Russian bears—convincingly from Wrenn, who was later to write perceptively on Pasternak. Wrenn left Oxford in 1939 for the Chair at King's College, London, returning only on Tolkien's exchanging the Oxford Anglo-Saxon Chair for the Merton English Language one. I recall helping Tolkien shelve some of his books, piled high and haphazardly ("a Belsen of books" he said ruefully) on the floor of a decidedly small room in Merton. Wrenn, however, had persuaded Pembroke to allot him a fine first-floor room in the front Quad; and this provoked in Tolkien a degree of jocular derision—not only for Wrenn the room-getter but for Wrenn's increasing (and effectual) part in Pembroke's affairs. One more aspect, of course, of that urbane aversion which characterised an older run of English scholars—mere industry too easily caricatured as wheeling and dealing. Well, let me guard against one misapprehension. Time loftily saved was not devoted to increasing an academic publication-list. We had to wait until 1936 for Tolkien's lively Academy lecture "*Beowulf*: the Monsters and the Critics", longer for Wrenn's little book on the English Language; and longer still for Wrenn's edition of *Beowulf*.

For his part, Wrenn unreservedly praised Tolkien; "genius" was the word that came oftenest from him. But the rift widened. One dreadful day I had walked with Tolkien through Christ Church Meadow, and he suggested we look in at the Examination Schools to see if his son Christopher's final results were posted. They were. Tolkien bent agonisingly before the notice-board, his face contorted, the right hand clenched above his head. "My poor Christopher" was all he could say, and he repeated it, a true *ululatus*, the unforced cry of primitive lament. It was soon over, but as unforgettable as that cry from Merlin which showed Ransom (in *That Hideous Strength*) "the whole character of the two-sided society in which this man must have lived". Tolkien, truly, had his being in two worlds, and there could be no proportion in his grief. Wrenn had been Chairman of the Examining Board, and, thinking to play some sort of peacemaker, I gathered that the examiners had praised Christopher for his brilliance in translation. I passed this on: but nothing would help. Tolkien mourned and would not be comforted: for his habitually mild and benevolently quizzical temper was capable of absolutely volcanic upheaval. Once, at the Newman centenary celebrations in Dublin, when Tolkien was honoured with the award of the D.Litt., I greeted him with an effort at the mild irony which characterised his own gentle repertoire. Dreadful mistake! I know what it is to be instantly rounded on, doomed in a moment to hasty retreat. What occasioned the outburst I still do not know. But on a later and more public occasion all was devastatingly clear.

I go back to Wrenn. His energy and effectiveness brought him an increasingly wide acquaintance among English scholars overseas. This led to a meeting, in 1950, at Magdalen, of Professors of English world-wide, and from this sprang the International Association of University Professors of English (IAUPE) which today has a membership of six hundred or so, distributed among thirty-five countries. More than anyone else, Wrenn can be credited with that achievement. It was carried to a successful conclusion notwithstanding bouts of dangerous illness, one requiring hospitalisation on the very eve of the Conference, and despite the indifference and even scepticism of Tolkien, who saw little merit in academics getting together. He was to boil over in spectacular style.

Wrenn's custom throughout the evenings of the Conference was to invite to the High Table in Magdalen those members who had been particularly helpful in arranging and conducting matters, leading them back after dinner for coffee and something stronger in the Conference office—the ground floor of St. Swithun's. Comfortably seated and contentedly gathered around Wrenn, the participants heard the door thrown open and a wild-eyed Tolkien—veritably "tollkühn", the foolhardy one—burst in, to harangue Wrenn for his unseemly action in so using Magdalen's High Table, to the neglect, it seemed of his fellow-Professors in Oxford. Here, burning alive, was that Hohenzollern who had broken in upon the stronghold of the Turk, to snatch the Sultan's standard. Speechless at last, stammering as he subsided, Tolkien glared in outrage at the astonished company. Was this the time or the place?, Wrenn murmured. Tolkien flung out and came no more to any Conference proceeding.

This awesome figure was essentially a solitary man, gravely put out by the stridency that sometimes seemed inseparable from meetings of the Inklings and was certainly predominant at the Eagle and Child gatherings on Tuesday mornings. He and Lewis, both, were strikingly indifferent to their surroundings. Tolkien found Auden's reference to his house in Sandfield Road as "hideous" not so much unacceptable (it was certainly that) as irrelevant. Similarly, John Betjeman's account of Lewis's Magdalen rooms as "arid" did no lasting harm, for it was felt to be merely imperceptive. Tolkien was content to make an office out of his garage. But *noise*—there was something hideously intrusive in that, and after Tolkien moved from the spaciousness of Northmoor Road he grew increasingly resentful of the invasion of privacy, the threat overshadowing any quiet reflection necessary to the steady writing and re-writing of his great prose work, a task which he regarded not as invention but as a form of historical recording. One day when he was living in Manor Road, seeing him so decidedly unhappy, I asked him when he had last read *The Silent Woman*. He replied by telling me of his midnight conversation with a long-distance lorry-driver who, like many of his fellows, chose to enter Oxford and park in or near Manor Road—finding it an agreeable change from slogging along the uninteresting by-pass which protectively encircled the sleeping University city. What, Tolkien asked despairingly, could one do with that degree of innocent offence?

Tolkien did however like the jaunts to Ireland which his

duties as External Examiner to the National University posi-
tively required—first to Dublin, then Maynooth, and so to Cork
and Galway. Like Lewis, he had travelled very little outside
mainland Britain, except (again, in both cases) for wartime
service in France. But he loved talk between one friend and
another when it turned to travel across the sea. I recall telling him of summers spent among deep-sea fishermen in trawl-
ers out of Milford Haven, with landfalls, expected and
unexpected, in South West Ireland. There are, obviously, links
with the solitary, expatriate boy, brought to England from his
birthplace in South Africa, and haunted by the Welsh names
on the side of coal-trucks passing through Birmingham. What
befell him in a far-off country, wartime France, we do not know.
The extinction of his battalion at Chemin des Dames found
him on the sidelines in England, disabled by trench-fever. His
admiration was forever undimmed when it turned to the
unforced decencies of the common man; the infantry soldier
of that First War metamorphosed into his own Sam Gamgee.

The wonderfully pleasing thing, above all, about such a
man was his unfeigned innocence—above all, of his own
standing. I remember that, one year, I sent him as a birthday
present a little nineteenth-century selection from Chaucer. His
surprise was unequalled: how did I know the date of his birth?
It was typical of him not to remember that there were such
compilations as *Who's Who*—even more, not to suppose that
his name would be recorded. There was, too, the unforcedly
beautiful script which served for every occasion; the unfailing courtesy which brought him to doff his cap whomever he
greeted; and the ready understanding he gave to the human
side of a relationship—so very, very different from Lewis's
awkward aloofness based on the assumption that impersonality was to be valued—on both sides—before all else.

Tolkien was directly instrumental in my first appointment—a venture, for both the Colleges concerned, into the uncharted waters of English studies. Meditating on the salary I was very ready to accept, he said pensively that a married man with two young children really needed a thousand pounds. Dazzling prospect (not to be realised for many a year!) but entirely typical coming from a man with a thriving family—and utterly unlike anything that would remotely occur to any others among the dons of that day, where decent reticence at all costs kept its distance. I think of that Magdalen don who would not leave the Common Room until in the small hours the last guest struggled to his feet, mumbling his regret at having to go. "Must you?" said his punctilious host; then added, "As a matter of fact, I must, too." Then, quickly and apologetically, "You see I was married this morning—I mean, yesterday." *Noblesse* carries its own obligations: above all, never to prefer its own interest.

As to the earlier friendship between Lewis and Tolkien, both were unworldly men, living innocently though not without a hostility easily aroused by the world they saw as irreversibly declining around them. Tolkien's sense of the quotidian realities ("a thousand pounds"") came from a devoted family life. He, too, had marked School Certificate examination papers. He liked to tell how he had been advanced from a "clerk" (his description) working on the Oxford English Dictionary to the eminence of a Chair—a postcard, he used to say, from Henry Bradley turned the scale: "Mr. Tolkien knows more Anglo-Saxon than any other man of his years." So a comparative affluence, one could fairly say, was his early lot. But devotion to a growing family kept him only too well aware of life's necessities: and when the children grew up it was time to withdraw from the relative affluence of Northmoor

Road to simpler settings (the Manor Road dwelling he described cheerfully as "a Scout's house"), moving eventually to the nondescript setting of Sandfield Road—and, of course, the solitary workplace of its adapted garage.

All this while, Lewis went on uninterruptedly at the Headington house he and his brother, retired from the peacetime Army, together with Mrs. Moore, mother of Lewis's wartime friend killed in the trenches, had bought as a joint venture those many years before. It was not a home in any but the simplest sense, rather a base from which Lewis the bachelor would sally forth into the wholly masculine society of his Oxford friends. It caused Tolkien some irritation that Lewis would on occasion chide him for having to return home. The ever-clamant society of the Bird and Baby, no less than the sometimes tumultuous exchanges of the Inklings, were decidedly not to Tolkien's taste. Lewis himself would readily respond to the trumpet, giving back in volume no less than cogency in at least the measure he had received.

A word must be said on that curious figure, Hugo Dyson. Here was another ex-Infantry Officer, voluble in the extreme, but absolute master of a devastating put-down. He was also, in those ostensibly literary gatherings, one of the least inclined to take pen in hand. Only a small book in an unambitious series lay to his credit. So he was the first to use both his vocal powers and his ever-ready wit to distract and to divert when talk became too closely literary for his taste. Twisting endlessly a piece of string in restless hands, he could pounce with unerring skill. The only forewarning was unaccustomed silence: then the deadly explosion. The gentle Bonamy Dobree, dining at Merton, resisted all Hugo's darts and flourishes; until Hugo, sulkily withdrawn, turned to deliver him up to posterity: "Oh, come on Dobree, admit it: you're all balls and *bon-*

homie". Such unerring skill was always in readiness; and when I think of the quiet ones among the Inklings—Colin Hardie, most reserved of men; David Cecil, a listener rather than a talker, but ready with spluttering approval of any sally that punctured momentary silence—then I can well understand Tolkien's growing disinclination to accept his friend Lewis in this setting.

There was a more unsettling figure. Wartime had brought Charles Williams to Oxford. Lewis and he had formed a friendship which, in Lewis's phrase, now "grew inward to the bone". Tolkien regarded Williams with a kindly tolerance; but the effect on Lewis was to encourage in him the strain of "science-fiction" first evident in the novel *Out of the Silent Planet* (1938). Williams's works were once described as "spiritual shockers", offering ventures into the mystical which culminate in a truly arcane conception of a Byzantium which contains the realm of Logres, where Athurian story is given a strange lustre. A measure of the distance Lewis travelled under Williams's influence is the contrast between the strong simplicities of Lewis's first two novels, *Out of the Silent Planet* and the incomparable *Perelandra* (where the threat of another Fall is to be averted), with, in the third novel the striking mixture of Senior Common Room jealousies and *naïvetés* set against a Merlin risen from the dead and a zoo of wild creatures in the end let loose to tear down a technology driven by outright devilry. This novel, *That Hideous Strength* (1945), was the last instance of Lewis's employment of a kind of science-fiction to establish eternal verities. I consider Lewis's science-fiction more fully in a later chapter. For the present, it is enough to say that where Tolkien was concerned, no great harm was done, though there was the annoying misappropriation of "Numinor" in the generous acknowledgement to "my friend Professor J. R. R.

Tolkien". But Lewis's very facility was, I do believe, peculiarly unsettling for Tolkien. On the one side, you had in Lewis a man of matchless clarity and force in all but effortless writing. Tolkien, on the other hand, was one who truly laboured at his appointed task. I do not mean that the result is laborious. But I do mean that Tolkien felt himself to be under a duty—as I have said, not to invent but to record. Lewis would, I believe, have thought this more like a deviation from real duty in any overriding sense. He once told me that he was what might be called a "first-time" writer, in the sense that we speak of "first-time" gifts in a games-player—no hesitation, the stroke delivered with perfect immediacy. I write one draft, he used to say; then I read it through and correct it; and then if I don't like it, away it goes into the wastepaper basket.

Lewis turned from his own form of science-fiction to the wholly new world of Narnia: and the ease with which he wrote marks a final transition from the world buried deep "in the manuscripts" of his friend. If Tolkien could not grasp how readily Lewis could write, Lewis could hardly understand how reluctant Tolkien was to publish. Once again I come to the vital distinction—that for Tolkien it was a task to record ancient truth: for Lewis invention was never taken for truth-telling of that order, though the archetypes of redemptive sacrifice and the restoration of lost happiness inform the *Chronicles of Narnia* at every turn. It is perhaps ironic that it was Tolkien who coined the just phrase for the essential characteristic of this kind of story-telling—its deployment of *eucatastrophe*, the turning to final happiness. There was, again, the essential difference between Catholic and Protestant—and at that, the Ulster Protestant. Lewis found his way back to Mother Kirk—not to any high ecclesiastical concept, but to a stubborn perseverance, a willed obedience its keynote. Truly, and literally, it was a regress. The forensics of his expositions of what he took to be *mere* (i.e., simple, unadulterated) Christianity have often enough been dwelt on—by his friends in the past—for instance, Farrer in *Light on C. S. Lewis* (1965): "His readers rub their eyes . . ." and, more recently, in A. N. Wilson's perceptive chapter on *Regress*. The sturdy, knock-down style of affirmation came out, sometimes startlingly, in speech. I once heard him calmly refer to a priest from Maynooth "who of course knew as much about theology as a pig". One looked in vain for an Orange-parodying irony. No, he meant it. The best passages in Lewis's religious writings take us to a level of sublimity—"the darling theme", as Farrer rightly calls it, of transcendent joy. But these are rare; they perhaps come too close to the "pi-jaw", the boy in Lewis lastingly turned from. Anyone seeking to measure the distance between Lewis and Tolkien (who, it will be remembered, played a distinctive part in Lewis's conversion), should lay down Lewis's Christian apologetics and read again the letter in which Tolkien gravely and tenderly expounds the concept of the Light of God to his son.

In summoning these remembrances from time now long past, I have incurred, no doubt, the charge of triviality. Lewis, it will be recalled, stoutly rebutted what he termed "The Personal Heresy". To it, on the purely literary level, I would reply that it overlooks (or, characteristically with Lewis, overrides) that vital third thing, neither merely biographical nor self-sufficiently aesthetic, but legitimately an object of critical attention—the writer *in* the work. To this I return in a later chapter. However that may be, it comforts me to recall in the present context Lewis's insistence on "every wrinkle, every stammer" in a friend; or, again, his recollection of a friend's dream in which Falstaff had appeared but alas! shorn of his fatness. Tolkien and Lewis—these are two men to be loved this side of idolatry and their very idiosyncrasies are venerable. Lewis departed once, to my astonishment, even incredulity, from his habitual mode. Waiting for him, at Magdalene's pub, The Pickerel, I saw advancing an unmistakably bulky figure—but one wearing, wonder of wonders, incontrovertibly a *suit*, neatly-pressed and in a decorously dark shade. An even greater surprise was in store. When asked what he would have, he replied, "A dry Martini". Even now I am inclined to disbelieve this strangest of apparitions and allocutions. Joy had for the moment worked a transformation on her bear.

Henry Bradley once dwelt on the paradox that a suit that would and one that would not "wear" could in English usage be one and the same. This suit at any rate, in the simplest sense, didn't wear. The last time I saw Lewis he was back in the familiar garb of baggy jacket and flannel trousers. It was a week before he died, and now the two brothers were together once more in the simplicity of the End Room, the safe surroundings of the Headington house where Warnie made the tea and tapped away at the typewriter. The books were fewer (a number had arrived almost surreptitiously at Blackwell's not long before). Lewis had not changed; but he was, for once, quieter. I remember we talked of Traherne; and I who had brought a copy of *Surprised by Joy* left it in the car, feeling that to ask him to sign it would have spoilt the innocence of a quiet conversation. I was reminded then, as I am now, of that passage where he speaks of "treasures of meekness" that may be drawn from those in a last illness. The depth of his suffering at Joy's death became public knowledge with the publication of *A Grief Observed* (1961). Here, under the pseudonym N. W. Clerk, the author of the buoyantly resolute *Problem of Pain* now set out with dogged clarity the problem of experienced desolation.

He once told me that when writing *The Problem of Pain* he had slipped in the bath, bruising a rib. Now he knew the misery of utter loss—and, good man, set himself to chart it.

It is widely known how the pseudonym N. W. Clerk—"Nat Whilk" ("I know not who")—was penetrated. But perhaps not so well known that the typescript had arrived in Faber & Faber's office on the strict understanding that no attempt should be made to penetrate the *nom de guerre*. It was T. S. Eliot, immediately sympathetic to the content, who was curious to know the author's identity, and Charles Monteith, an Ulsterman who had read English at Magdalen in a shortened course before departing for War Service, was at hand to make the identification. Lewis's handwriting, evident in corrections to the typescript, was simple, nearly print-like, a script almost perfectly anonymous, a means simply of transmission. I think of *A Grief Observed* as truly indicative of Lewis—for its truth-telling in the depth of adversity (one recalls his admiration for Scott refusing to submit when in the very pit of misery); and, more humbly, for the authenticity of its having been written in the blank pages of an exercise book containing some "ancient arithmetic". Indelibly, there is the Lewis I met once a week for the three years of my tutorials, driving a steel-nibbed pen across the page until it had to be laid aside. "You may make a writer or a scholar of him, but you'll not make anything else. You may make up your mind to *that*." Thus Kirk, his old mentor, reporting to Lewis's father: and a writer, I shall later argue, he remained. *Quellenforschung* never dominated the impulse to communicate vividly and memorably.

The news of Lewis's death came to me in a lay-by outside Newbury, where I stopped to read the Sunday newspaper picked up and unopened that morning. All that day in Winchester, the ancient capital tantalisingly linked with Malory,

I kept recalling Jack Lewis in the sheer individuality of his being—the unity in diversity of reason, an indomitable will to comprehend, and romance, the unending awareness of something never perfectly given in waking consciousness.

The funeral was a very quiet affair. Only a few of Lewis's closest friends were there; his brother, quite overcome, not among the company. I found only one I could speak to— Tolkien, to my eyes more youthful and vigorous than ever. He spoke of Lewis's leaving too late an operation to cure his "old man's trouble" almost as though this were simply negligence on Lewis's part. No doubt, to some extent it was. A. N. Wilson has dealt unsparingly with Dr. Havard, the Useless Quack. But I think I see something of the stoical contempt for illness that was, in Lewis, paradoxically balanced with that ideal of nursery happiness best expressed in *The Allegory of Love*. Ending his account of the Italian romance epic he wrote of the "ideal happiness . . . to be always convalescent from some small illness and always seated in a window that overlooked the sea, there to read these poems eight hours of each happy day". Certainly I was not alone in experiencing a frustration that easily shaded into annoyance when, each Hilary Term, Lewis would retire to Headington for a fortnight or so, handing over his small tutorial flock to extemporised help. So I cannot imagine a doctor having a more docile patient if it was a matter of bed-rest and punctual cups of tea. But, equally, there could scarcely be a less attentive listener if, this time, there might be a prospect of dying.

As I write, Mount's Bay lies in view, offering an external parallel to that setting which, in his interior world, was Lewis's place of deepest longing, bringing the sense of that Island from which enticing winds blew, to draw John the Pilgrim onward. Though both Lewis and Tolkien were markedly untravelled men, and each could sit contentedly in severely uninspiring surroundings, yet each had an unfailing light within. Tolkien could make his way back to that garage in Sandfield Road and dwell in the undiminished light of the world he chronicled. In his little inner room at Magdalen, a good retreat when winter was drawing in, Lewis had on the wall a framed landscape commonplace in itself save for bare branches lit by—yes, a "green light that lingers in the West". For Coleridge, it was a light that devastated: his was a realised and irretrievable loss—

> *I may not hope from outward forms to win*
> *The passion and the life, whose fountains are within.*

But for Lewis, as for Tolkien, there could be no ground of disappointment, much less despair. The surge of imagination was not to be challenged by, and therefore could never be made subordinate to, external Nature. Rather, the light by which each lived was drawn from a remembered vision, renewed on each revisiting. For each of these untravelled men it was, before all else, the sea that held the unrivalled challenge. Each has left a characteristic glimpse of the highest intensity, and equally, of an unforced calm.

Tolkien concludes his assault on the purposeless excavations of scholarship, at the outset of his British Academy Lecture, "*Beowulf: the Monsters and the Critics*", thus:

> So they pushed the tower over, with no little labour, in order to look for hidden carvings and inscriptions, or to discover whence the man's distant forefathers had obtained their building material. Some suspecting a deposit of coal under the soil began to dig for it, and forgot even the stones. They all said: "This tower is most interesting." But they also said (after pushing it over): "What a muddle it is in!" And even the man's own descendants, who might have been expected to consider what he had been about, were heard to murmur: "He is such an odd

fellow! Imagine his using these old stones just to build a nonsensical tower! Why did he not restore the old house? He had no sense of proportion." But from the top of that tower the man had been able to look out upon the sea.

When, many years later, the long labour of *The Lord of the Rings* was to be concluded, only an epilogue, told by that unassuming character, Sam Gamgee, could serve to bring all into focus. A fitting end is made when, all speech done, we hear "the sigh and murmur of the Sea upon the shores of Middle-earth".

Lewis, that equally home-keeping man, reflects a hundred night crossings of the Irish Sea in a passage which Coghill especially admired. It is from Lewis's last book, and shows an unabated (and, surely, still unrivalled) expository power. Lewis takes his reader to the heart of a discarded image:

> Whatever else a modern feels when he looks at the night sky, he certainly feels that he is looking *out*—like one looking out from the saloon entrance on to the dark Atlantic or from the lighted porch upon dark and lonely moors. But if you accepted the Medieval Model you would feel like one looking *in*. The Earth is "outside the city wall". When the sun is up he dazzles us and we cannot see inside. Darkness, our own darkness, draws the veil and we catch a glimpse of the high pomps within; the vast, lighted concavity filled with music and life.

There an unchanging, even prosaic, external prospect is brilliantly turned to account. Nature, the old tag runs, makes nothing in vain. These two masters neglect no part of ordinary experience in showing forth complex truth. It is the greatest of gifts; and it finds expression in an unmatched simplicity of language.

ILLUSTRATIONS

Oct 4 / 56

Dear John — Thanks very much. The Thos. A. Kemp-
-age is a gem of domest-ray. I haven't the sermons;
I meet them in the spare room of a house I some-
-times stay at. By the way, my medieval mission
at Cambridge is, so far, a _flop d'estime_. A few
dons come to my lectures but far fewer under-
-grads. I've never had such small audiences be-
-fore. Must be frightfully good for me. But your
project about texts is already under weigh —
see the enclosed. Brewer, as you probably know,
was a Magdalen man (much junior to you). My
brother joins me in greetings and in thanks for your
almost Homeric offer of hospitality. Can we

thing, dog, cat, secretary, chauffeur, concubines, two valets, and a gentleman usher! (Of course you have adequate stabling for the horses?) But do come to Magdalene.

Yours

Jack

"... my medieval mission at Cambridge is, so far, a *flop d'estime*" (p. 13). The "Homeric offer" was simply an invitation that he and Warnie might come and stay for a while.

31 Aug 62

The Kilns,
Headington Quarry,
Oxford

I have been ill for a long time but am now v. much better, tho' still strictly dieted and cautious about stairs. But quite well enough to read a book by you, even one about P. Plowman.

J.

A characteristic reponse to the suggestion that he might like the present of a book.

7 Nov. 52

Dear John

I am touched by your suggestion. If I've
done my arithmetic right 1966 will be the year of
my retirement. Of course I'd enjoy so great an
honour, but the really important question is whether
there are a sufficient number of people who want to
write something and can find such a _Festschrift_ a
good VENT for it. If it is that way round, if
the occasion acts as midwife rather than as father
to the essays, a F. may be a useful book. But if it's
the other way, if people have to find a subject because
they are asked to contribute to the F. then it leads
scholars to waste their time. You see? So I can
only leave the matter entirely to you. A dinner
would be better for the older, but not for me
who am allowed to eat almost nothing. I suppose
the head of F.R.Leavis in a charger would be
rather too worldly?

Whatever comes of it I shall always value

*myself the more because you had the idea.
I have praise of your P. P. Look,*

*yours
Jack*

Responding to the news that a *Festschrift* was being prepared:
"I suppose the head of F. R. Leavis in a charger
would be rather too costly?"

56/383

The Kilns,Kiln Lane,
Headington Quarry,
Oxford.
Ist October I956.

Dear John,

        Hang it,I've about shot my bolt on Milton and don't really
want to deal with the recent critics. My finger grows weary of hornet's
nests. Also I'm trying to learn a little about the Middle Ages. There
are so many things one handed over to the Language people at Oxford
which I have to talk about at Cambridge.
My brother joins me in good wishes. Letters between you and I have
crossed,have'nt they?

Yours,

Jack

"My finger grows weary of hornet's nests." (p. 116).
A cheerfully ungrammatical note.

Annotations of *Revelations of Divine Love* by Julian of Norwich,
which Lewis was reading in the summer of 1940 (p. 30).
The last page of the book is inscribed "11 Aug 1940".

Sin has no substance and is real only in the pain it causes.

56 REVELATIONS OF DIVINE LOVE

much to be forsaken, but nevertheless mourning and
sorrow I made therefor, without reason and discretion.

But Jesus, who in this Vision informed me of all that
is needful to me, answered by this word and said : *It
behoved that there should be sin ;* [1] *but all shall be well, and all
shall be well, and all manner of thing shall be well.*

In this naked word *sin*, our Lord brought to my
mind, generally, *all that is not good*, and the shameful
despite and the utter noughting [2] that He bare for us in
this life, and His dying ; and all the pains and passions
of all His creatures, ghostly and bodily ; (for we be
all partly noughted, and we shall be noughted following
our Master, Jesus, till we be full purged, that is to say,
till we be fully noughted of our deadly flesh and of all
our inward affections which are not very good ;) and the
beholding of this, with all pains that ever were or ever
shall be,—and with all these I understand the Passion
of Christ for most pain, and overpassing. All this was
shewed in a touch and quickly passed over into comfort :
for our good Lord would not that the soul were affeared
of this terrible sight.

Cf. λ. 112.

But I saw not *sin*: for I believe it hath no manner of
substance nor no part of being, nor could it be known
but by the pain it is cause of.

3

And thus [3] pain, *it* is something, as to my sight, for a
time ; for it purgeth, and maketh us to know ourselves
and to ask mercy. For the Passion of our Lord is comfort to us against all this, and so is His blessed will.

[1] "Synne is behovabil, but al shal be wel & al shal be wel & al
manner of thyng shal be wele."

[2] Being made as nothing, set at nought.

[3] S. de Cressy has " this " instead of *thus*.

Line 5: "All shall be well, and all shall be well, and all manner of
thing shall be well" is quoted in *A Grief Observed*.

THE THIRTEENTH REVELATION 57

And for the tender love that our good Lord hath to all that shall be saved, He comforteth readily and sweetly, signifying thus: *It is sooth*[1] *that sin is cause of all this pain; but all shall be well, and all shall be well, and all manner [of] thing shall be well.*

These words were said full tenderly, showing no manner of blame to me nor to any that shall be saved. Then were it a great unkindness[2] to blame or wonder on God for my sin, since He blameth not me for sin.

And in these words I saw a marvellous high mystery hid in God, which mystery He shall openly make known to us in Heaven: in which knowing we shall verily see the cause why He suffered sin to come. In which sight we shall endlessly joy in our Lord God.[3]

---

[1] *i.e.* truth, an actual reality. See lxxxii.

[2] As it were, an unreasonable contravention of natural, filial trust.

[3] See also chap. lxi. From the *Enchiridion* of Saint Augustine:—
"All things that exist, therefore, seeing that the Creator of them all is supremely good, are themselves good. But because they are not like their Creator, supremely and unchangeably good, their good may be diminished and increased. But for good to be diminished is an evil, although, however much it may be diminished, it is necessary, if the being is to continue, that some good should remain to constitute the being. For however small or of whatever kind the being may be, the good which makes it a being cannot be destroyed without destroying the being itself. . . So long as a being is in process of corruption, there is in it some good of which it is being deprived; and if a part of the being should remain which cannot be corrupted, this will certainly be an incorruptible being, and accordingly the process of corruption will result in the manifestation of this great good. But if it do not cease to be corrupted, neither can it cease to possess good of which corruption may deprive it. But if it should be thoroughly and completely consumed by corruption, there will then be no good left, because there will be no being. Wherefore corruption can consume the good only by consuming the being. Every being, therefore, is a good; a great good, if it cannot be corrupted; a little good, if it can:

Headline: "Since God does not blame *us* for sin, it would be hard if *we* blamed *Him!*" This remark catches Lewis's characteristic tone.

But in the higher part (signified by the "inward regard") there are no mercies nor pardons but only joy. ①

126 REVELATIONS OF DIVINE LOVE

shewed in the [Lord's] *outward* manner of Regard.   In which shewing I saw *two* parts : the one is the rueful falling of man, the other is the worshipful Satisfaction [1] that our Lord hath made for man.

cf. p. 131.

The other manner of Regard was shewed *inward*: and that was more highly and all [fully] *one*.[2]   For the life and the virtue that we have in the lower part is of the higher, and it cometh down to us [from out] of the Natural love of the [high] Self, by [the working of] grace. Atwix [the life of] the one and [the life of] the other there is right nought: for it is all one love.   Which one blessed love hath now, in us, double working : for in the lower part are pains and passions, mercies and forgiveness, and such other that are profitable ; but in the higher part are none of these, but all one high love and marvellous joy: in [3] which joy all pains are highly restored.   And in this [time] our Lord showed not only our Excusing [4] [from blame, in His beholding of our higher part], but the worshipful nobility that He shall bring us to [by the working of grace in our lower part], turning all our blame [that is therein, from our falling] into endless worship [when we be oned to the high Self above]. [5]

[1] " Asseth."

[2] " and al on "—perhaps for *all is one.*

[3] " in " = *in, into,* or *unto.*

[4] *i.e. Exculpating*—as in Romans ii. 15.

[5] " Man,—seeing he is not a simple nature—in one aspect of his being, which is the better, and that I may speak more openly what I ought to speak, his very self, is immortal ; but on the other side, which is weak and fallen, and which alone is known to those who have no faith except in sensible things, he is obnoxious to mortality and mutability."—From the *Didascolon* of Hugo of St Victor, as quoted in F. D. Maurice's *Mediæval Philosophy*, p. 147.

① *I am v. doubtful whether I understand this page.*

② *Natural means almost the opposite to what we mean by it in the antithesis "Spiritual X Natural". It means "pertaining to our real or transcendental substance", as opposed to our "sensuality" cf pp. 131, 132, 136 n 3 (where god is kyndhede) 138, 156.*

Note 1: "I am v. doubtful whether I understand this page."

Thus man can be blameworthy quâ his lower self and blameless in his Real Will, which is in Christ.

CHAPTER LIII

"In every soul that shall be saved is a Godly Will that never assented to sin, nor ever shall." "Ere that He made us He loved us, and when we were made we loved Him"

AND I saw that He willeth that we understand He taketh not harder the falling of any creature that shall be saved than He took the falling of Adam, which, we know, was endlessly loved and securely kept in the time of all his need, and now is blissfully restored in high overpassing joy. For our Lord is so good, so gentle, and so courteous, that He may never assign default [in those] in whom He shall ever be blessed and praised.

And in this that I have now told was my desire in part answered, and my great difficulty[1] some deal eased, by the lovely, gracious Shewing of our good Lord. In which Shewing I saw and understood full surely that in every soul that shall be saved is a Godly Will that never assented to sin, nor ever shall : which Will is so good that it may never will evil, but evermore continually it willeth good ; and worketh good in the sight of God. Therefore our Lord willeth that we know this in the Faith and the belief ; and especially that we have all this blessed Will whole and safe in our Lord Jesus Christ. For that same Kind[2] that Heaven shall be filled with behoveth needs, of God's rightfulness, so to have been knit and oned to Him, that therein was kept a Sub-

H. 105, 106

[1] "awer "=awe, travail of perplexity, dilemma—see p. 106.
[2] Man's nature.

178 REVELATIONS OF DIVINE LOVE

and Grace; the third is that we know meekly what our self is anent our sin and feebleness. And for these three was all the Shewing made, as to mine understanding.

CHAPTER LXXIII

"Two manners of sickness that we have: impatience, or sloth;—despair, or mistrustful dread"

ALL the blessed teaching of our Lord was shewed by three parts: that is to say, by bodily sight, and by word formed in mine understanding, and by spiritual sight. For the bodily sight, I have said as I saw, as truly as I can; and for the words, I have said them right as our Lord shewed them to me; and for the spiritual sight, I have told some deal, but I may never fully tell it: and therefore of this sight I am stirred to say more, as God will give me grace.

God shewed two manners of sickness that we have: the one is impatience, or sloth: for we bear our travail and our pains heavily; the other is despair, or doubtful dread, which I shall speak of after. *Generally*, He shewed *sin*, wherein that all is comprehended, but in special He shewed only these two. And these two are they that most do travail and tempest us, according to that which our Lord shewed me; and of them He would have us be amended. I speak of such men and women as for God's love hate sin and dispose themselves to do God's will (a) then by our spiritual blindness and bodily heaviness we are most inclining to these. And therefore

(a) N.B. The whole book deals with those who have already reached a pretty high degree of sanctity. It wd. be rash to apply most of it directly to ones own problems.

Headline: "The doctrine here developed has special reference (a) to impatience or Sloth (b) to Despair."

SUNDRY TEACHINGS   179

it is God's will that they be known, for then we shall refuse them as we do other sins.

And for help of this, full meekly our Lord shewed the patience that He had in His Hard Passion; and also the joying and the satisfying that He hath of that Passion, for love.   And this He shewed in example that we should gladly and wisely bear our pains, for that is great pleasing to Him and endless profit to us.   And the cause why we are travailed with them is for lack in knowing[1] of Love.   Though the three Persons in the Trinity[2] be all even[3] in Itself, the soul[4] took most understanding in Love; yea, and He willeth that in all things we have our beholding and our enjoying in Love.   And of 'this knowing are we most blind.   For some of us believe that God is Almighty and may do all, and that He is All-Wisdom and can do all; but that He is All-Love and will do all, there we stop short.[5]   And this not-knowing it is, that hindereth most God's lovers, as to my sight.

For when we begin to hate sin, and amend us by the ordinance of Holy Church, yet there dwelleth a dread that letteth us, because of the beholding of our self and of our sins afore done.   And some of us because of our every-daily sins: for we hold not our Covenants, nor keep we our cleanness that our Lord setteth us in, but fall oftentimes into so much wretchedness that shame it is to see it.   And the beholding of this maketh us so sorry and so heavy, that scarsely we can find any comfort.

And this dread we take sometime for a meekness, but it is a foul blindness and a weakness.[6]   And we cannot

---

[1] " for *unknowing*."   [2] seen as Might, Wisdom, Love.   [3] *i.e.* equal.
[4] *i.e.* Julian (xiii., xxiv., xlvi.).   [5] "astynten."
[6] S. de Cressy: "a wickedness"; but the MS. word is "waykenes."

① v. ʱʱ *143-145*.
② A good illustration of the meanings of *mazan* and *cunnan*.

Headline: The masquerade of meekness "really a fault".
Note 1: *Mazan* and *cunnan* are to be distinguished.

PART II

REFLECTIONS

4

Interplanetary Voyaging

LEWIS'S INTEREST IN SCIENCE-FICTION (he earlier preferred the term "scientifiction") may be, in one sense, dated pretty precisely. In a letter written on 9 July 1939 we find: "what set me about writing the book (*Out of the Silent Planet*) was the discovery that a pupil of mine took all that dream of interplanetary colonization quite seriously . . . You will be both grieved and amused to hear that out of about 60 reviews only two showed any knowledge that my idea of the fall of the Bent One was anything but an invention of my own . . . any amount of theology can now be smuggled into people's minds under cover of romance without their knowing it".

Lewis has told us that he "had read fantastic fiction of all sorts ever since [he] could read"; and, more movingly, that "All my seven Narnian books, and my three science fiction books, began with seeing pictures in my head".

There is certainly no need to seek for any one moment of creation, much less any one dominant purpose. The form fell readily to his hand when he perceived, recording his debt to Lindsay's *Voyage to Arcturus*, "what other planets in fiction are really good for; for *spiritual* adventures. Only they can satisfy the craving which sends our imaginations off the earth."

Another aspect of this is revealed in a letter to Roger Lancelyn Green: "What immediately spurred me to write was Olaf Stapledon's *Last and First Men* and an essay ["The Last Judgment"] in J. B. S. Haldane's *Possible Worlds*, both of which seem to take the idea of such travel seriously and to have the desperately immoral outlook which I try to pillory in Weston. I like the whole planetary idea as a *mythology* and simply wished to conquer for my own Christian point of view what has always been used by the opposite side."

There we have not only the impulse to create, but also the argumentative force which sustains the writer: for in Lewis, before all else, there is an abundance of energy which manifests itself in both—to use an older critical terminology— reason and imagination. The fantasy is never at variance with the dialectical thrust—a truly unique combination.

Out of the Silent Planet was written in 1937 ("some time", says Walter Hooper, "between the spring and autumn"). The opening is firmly drawn. Ransom, the pedestrian, is an unpromising hero, and the landscape through which he trudges is equally barren of promise—"flat fields and a mass of darkness". But it is a moral obligation which keeps Ransom going, his promise to an old woman to do what he can for her unfortunate son; and so, unfitted for adventure as he may be, he is drawn in. Against his drabness and apparent ineffectuality the two main protagonists are shown in full relief. Weston, the master-scientist, is self-possessed—and perpetually irate. Devine is smooth, and endlessly devious. With Devine we sense the author's own awareness of inexplicable advancement in academic life—"wondering from afar how anyone so flashy and, as it were, ready-made could be so successful".

There are only two possible viewpoints: "A damn clever chap, Devine, in his own way", or else, "It's a mystery to me how that man has got where he is". At all events, Devine remains unchanged, the eternal malicious schoolboy, and it is he who sees the opportunity which has fallen into their lap and who, contriving an extra-terrestrial kidnapping, implants in Ransom the fear that he is being taken to Mars to be sacrificed to the dreaded *sorns*. So the progress of the book is Ransom's awaking to his true destiny; and in this process he has to be steadily corrected. He must lose his fears of "space" as coldness, darkness, and hostility; of the creatures who people his imagined universe—"horrors such as ancient and medieval mythology could hardly rival"; and, finally, he must shed his conviction that death is preferable to being handed over to "an extra-terrestrial Otherness". In a sense, we are repeating the theme of *The Pilgrim's Regress* (1933); an unlearning is the prior condition of advance. Ransom stealing the sharpest kitchen knife has determined, as he thinks, the only possible solution. But when he has made his escape from his captors, Ransom finds he has only liberated a flood of self-pity. In a most perceptive passage, at the end of chapter eight, Ransom feels "a sort of physical, almost a filial, love for his own body"; and the image of pure pathos is completed by the thought of "men going to bed on the far-distant planet Earth—men in clubs, and liners, and hotels, married men, and small children who slept with nurses in the room, and warm, tobacco-smelling men tumbled together in forecastles and dug-outs".

This vividly returns us to Lewis's first published work, *Spirits in Bondage* (1919)—a "Cycle of Lyrics" in three parts: "The Prison House; Hesitation; The Escape". There, too, the sustaining theme is a journey to a land of heart's desire:

> *In my coracle of verses I will sing of lands unknown,*
> *Flying from the scarlet city where a Lord that knows no*
>   *pity*
> *Mocks the broken people praying round his iron throne,*
> *—Sing about the Hidden Country fresh and full of quiet*
>   *green.*
> *Sailing over seas uncharted to a port that none has seen.*

But for the young poet there is an entire and frightening contrast between the desired landfall and the baleful authority of a God who is "very strong", holding "the keys of Hell". Reason itself seems to justify man in rebellion:

> *Yet I will not bow down to thee nor love thee*

and escape must be made. Twenty-two years later, the truth to which Ransom is brought entails a reversal not only of irrational fears of a potentially hostile Universe but, in the end, of the very human reluctance to be "drawn in". *Out of the Silent Planet* illustrates very well the continuing truth enunciated in the preface to the third edition of *Pilgrim's Regress* (1943). Man is to be required not simply to accept but, vividly and inescapably, to enact "a sort of ontological proof".

Ransom, then, must be led to know the beauties of Malacandra, and they start with the taste of its water and the discovery that the planet's vegetation can be eaten. His first headlong flight has "degenerated into an endless ramble", and this allows fuller description of the terrain; then of some of its inhabitants; and, in flight from a second glimpse of the dreaded *sorn*, there is the starting-point of change when Ransom comes upon his first *hross*. No retreat is now possible. Ransom "felt little emotion": "He noted in a dry, objective way that this was apparently to be the end of his story . . ." The transition is most deftly made. Ransom realises that the *hross* is *talking*. It has "articulate language". So Ransom the scholar is carried across the threshold, into new knowledge: "In the fraction of a second which it took Ransom to decide that the creature was really talking, and while he still knew that he might be facing instant death, his imagination had leaped over every fear and hope and probability of his situation to follow the dazzling project of making a Malacandrian grammar. *An Introduction to the Malacandrian Language—The Lunar Verb—A Concise Martian-English Dictionary* . . . the titles flitted through his mind."

There is a vivid parallel in an incident later in the trilogy, when the scientist Filostrato is, appallingly, beheaded. There, too, "the love of knowledge is a kind of madness". Filostrato "had even calculated what changes the terror of the victim would make in his blood pressure . . . His last thought was that he had underestimated the terror".

The process of educating Ransom is like that in the Fourth Book of *Gulliver's Travels*. Gulliver's meeting with his first Houyhnhnm is marked by the condescension of his attempt to fondle it, "using the common style of jockeys". But Gulliver must be drawn to reverence the Houyhnhnm; Ransom, in his turn, passes from intellectual excitement to unquestioning affection. But this is still a long way off when he hesitates to accept the *hross*'s invitation to accompany him on a journey. For Ransom's "whole imaginative training; linking the *hross* with the dreaded *sorn*", "somehow encouraged him to asso-ciate superhuman intelligence with monstrosity of form and ruthlessness of will". Yet Ransom has become attached to the *hross* "by bonds stronger than he knew"; so he steps into the boat and his education begins.

I believe that the long, skilful discourses between *hross* and man are the training-ground for the remarkable skill and cogency of Lewis's later religious broadcasts. Let me instance the *sorn*'s discourse on the nature of *eldila* where the ideas of light and speed are marvellously handled, so that we deal with things that "are not strange . . . though they are beyond our senses". For Ransom, as for the reader, the universe is turned "rather oddly inside out". The passage foreshadows that appeal to the reader's imagination which stands out in *The Discarded Image* (1964), when Earth itself is seen as "outside the city wall" and it is man's own darkness "which draws the veil". An unrivalled power of exposition is already evident as man and *sorn* discourse together.

Inseparable from this magistral gift is a vein of irony which, deftly counterpointing Ransom's progress, comes into full play when, at the conclusion of *Out of the Silent Planet*, Weston and Devine stand before Oyarsa, with Ransom as their interpreter. Weston and Devine speak a pidgin Malacandrian: "No, no, Oyarsa . . . You no listen to him. He very foolish man, he have dreams. We little people, only want pretty sun-bloods. You give us plenty sun-bloods, we go back into the sky, you never see us no more. All done, see?" It is wickedly funny, and of course it is not to everyone's taste. But for me it leads to a *tour de force*; for soon it is Weston's full, unhampered rhetoric that must be turned into what may be called Malacandrian true-speak. Weston's own measured speeches are Lewis the parodist at his best: "To you I may seem a vulgar robber, but I bear on my shoulders the destiny of the human race." Devastatingly, this becomes "Among us, Oyarsa, there is a kind of *hnau* who will take other *hnaus*' food and—and things, when they are not looking. He says he is not an ordinary one of that kind. He says what he does now will make very different things happen to those of our people who are not yet born." One is reminded of Gulliver's unquestioning assertion of "civilised" values before the King of Brobdingnag. But here on Malacandra the irony of situation is reinforced by the unshakeable need for true clarity in the translation.

Weston's peroration is noble: "I may fall . . . But while I live I will not, with such a key in my hand, consent to close the gates of the future on my race. What lies in that future, beyond our present ken, passes imagination to conceive: it is enough for me that there is a Beyond."

Ransom's translation is unequivocal: "He is saying . . . that he will not stop trying to do all this unless you kill him. And he says that though he doesn't know what will happen to the creatures who spring from us, he wants it to happen very much." This art, of irremediably puncturing high-flown speech, is one side of Lewis's gifts as parodist—one who, delighting in language, commands a formidable battery of skills. Perhaps its fullest deployment, as we shall see, is in *That Hideous Strength*, where the bureaucratic inanities of Wither, and the vacuous dreariness of Cosser, have a full play alongside Featherstone's suave rhetoric; and this in turn involves the self-flattering complicity of Mark Studdock in composing both broadsheet and tabloid "leaders" on disorders in Edgestow. But the single, sustained and most effective use of this skill is in Lewis's next work in the "science-fiction" mode, *Perelandra* (1943).

Lewis is on record as not having foreseen a sequel to *Out of the Silent Planet*. In *Perelandra* he himself appears as an agent in the story, and this enables him to express in his own person that deep-seated unwillingness to get "drawn in" which, no longer applicable to Ransom, is needed to give high-flying fiction a base in all too human fact. So, once again, the opening is a journey made with reluctance: "The thing was such sheer bad luck. Ransom himself had been taken to Mars (or Malacandra) against his will and almost by accident, and I had become connected with his affair by another accident. Yet here we were, both getting more and more involved in what I could only describe as inter-planetary politics." This time, in chapter one, it is truly a barrage the pedestrian must go through. Shaken to the point of near-hysteria, he arrives at his destination—only to find a frightening reversal of expectation. There is no finer ending to an opening chapter than this, when the traveller hears man and *eldil* speaking together. His feelings are "of resentment, horror, and jealousy. It was in my mind to shout out 'Leave your familiar alone, you damned magician, and attend to Me'.

"What I actually said was, 'Oh, Ransom. Thank God you've come'."

Perelandra is certainly Lewis's most ambitious undertaking. Nothing less is in prospect than a re-enactment of the First Temptation. This time the tempter is the scientist Weston, a notion immeasurably deepened when eventually, through Weston, a voice "louder and deeper than before" speaks. Once again, Ransom, the merely human opponent, finds it all "Unfair . . . unfair". How is he to fight when, once more, but this time with immeasurable consequences in the balance, he is "forbidden to lie and yet brought to places where truth seemed fatal"? Most insidiously, "How if the enemy were right after all? *Felix peccatum Adae*. Even the Church would tell him that good came of disobedience in the end." The spell is broken when the Lady asks Ransom if he agrees with his opponent: and then "the managed corpse, the bogey" is seen for what it is. It is an "Un-man", one who howls like a dog when the question is turned back on him—"What good came to you? Do *you* rejoice that Maleldil became a man?"

Throughout, Lewis holds fast to the truth of human reluctance to be involved. The mouse will not search for the cat. But involved Ransom is; the significance of his name is brought inescapably home—"a payment that delivers": and still "he bowed his head and groaned and repined against his fate to be still a man and yet to be forced up into the metaphysical world, to enact what philosophy only thinks". The *psychomachia* which follows is Lewis at his best. In the end, the question "Lord, why me?" is not answered but transcended: "The whole struggle was over, and yet there seemed to have been no moment of victory."

Lewis draws on his Boethius; in the *Consolation* the debate between freedom and constraint had been resolved by removing Divine knowledge altogether out of Time as man must experience it—as mere succession. Divide and sub-divide as we will, each nearly infinitesimal moment can only be perceived as preceding one and succeeding another. But God's knowledge can be conceived, in these terms, only as an eternal Present: "Past, present, future *He* beholds." So, for Ransom, "The thing was going to be done. There was going to arrive, in the course of time, a moment at which he would have done it. The future act stood there, fixed and unalterable as if he had already performed it. It was a mere irrelevant detail that it happened to occupy the position we call future instead of that which we call past." The conclusion is solidly Boethian: "Predestination and freedom were apparently identical. He could no longer see any meaning in the many arguments he had heard on this subject." What has to be done is now seen with final clarity. It is a struggle to the death. For Lewis the moralist "courage is every virtue at the breaking-point". So, against all probability, Man and Un-man must meet, hand to hand; and it is characteristic of Lewis's realism, his fidelity to humble fact, that there is nothing dignified, no trace of the heroic, in this struggle—merely the bodies of two middle-aged men grappling clumsily with each other, until in the end Ransom strikes the final, desperate blow, crying aloud: "In the name of the Father and of the Son and of the Holy Ghost, here goes—I mean, Amen."

The finale of the story is in one great assembly, where the King and Queen of a world now truly ransomed hold a levée which climaxes in a Great Dance. Here Lewis's mastery of styles mounts with assurance in a series of statements characterising triumphant paradox. Each utterance ends with the invocation "Blessed be He!"; each ascends to a final truth: "There seems no plan because it is all plan: there seems no centre because it is all centre." And, in the end: "this seeming also is the end and final cause for which He spreads out Time so long and Heaven so deep; lest if we never met the dark, and the road that leads no-whither, and the question to which no answer is imaginable, we should have in our minds no likeness of the Abyss of the Father, into which if a creature drop down his thoughts for ever he shall hear no echo return to him. Blessed, blessed, blessed be He!" Lewis's imagination is at full stretch in this extended epiphany. The measured rhythms of this exalted prose seem to me comparable with the lyrics of *The Pilgrim's Regress* in finding language for a profoundly religious yet wholly creative imagination, reaching out to encompass mystery upon mystery. *Perelandra* remains Lewis's most ambitious attempt to portray Deep Heaven itself—and more, that Final Cause which is all but unimaginably greater: and all this consistently in language which, above all exultant, is yet firmly concrete.

With *That Hideous Strength* (1945) we are uncompromisingly returned to Earth. It is too much for some critics. I remember, when the book first came out, reading in the *Times*

Literary Supplement a review which took Lewis sharply to task for a tale that lacked coherence and characters that failed to move away from pasteboard. I, on the contrary, find in this last work of the trilogy a freedom and energy that superbly command attention, and an ironic humour that stamps the authenticity of characters and setting. The chief protagonist is, again, *homme moyen*: but this time rather more worldly than before, a step farther in upon The Inner Ring, or, as they call it in Bracton College, the Progressive Element. Mark Studdock is no reluctant participant: he is very willing to be "drawn in". For the first time in the trilogy we trace a moral decline, the steps firmly characterised, and the setting depicted with an insider's knowledge of academic life. Devine—now Lord Feverstone—is Mark's mentor; and a truly horrid Fairy, a ruthless Chief of Police, his watchdog.

Lewis's classic theme of reluctance is this time focused upon Mark's wife, Jane, who, much against her will, is drawn into the little company that has gathered around Ransom, now disclosed as the Pendragon of Logres, alias Mr. Fisher-King. Jane is to be sympathised with: "It's rough luck on you", says Denniston, one of the small remnant of Logres: and he explains to his wife, "We are in fact asking her to take a leap in the dark". Jane is inescapably drawn in when her frightening dreams are to be seen less as *her* dreams and more—"well, as News". The battle is on, and the excitement rises when it becomes clear that each party—the vastly funded and ruthlessly well-equipped National Institute of Co-ordinated Experiments, over against Mr. Fisher-King's little band—is equally uncertain of the side to be taken by a Merlin newly risen from his fifteen centuries of slumber in the heart of Bragdon Wood. There is nothing more purely exhilarating in the trilogy than the thrill of the chase and the bringing to bay, first of the pseudo-Merlin—a scene rich in comedy as Wither and Frost pay deference to a wily old tramp—and the disclosure of the true Merlin, a figure of untamed arrogance, properly contemptuous at his first entrance into Ransom's house.

All Lewis's formidable skill in language, his delight in the expertise of matching word and cadence to speaker, rises to these twin occasions, paired as they are, diptych-fashion. In the one, Wither's windy and indeterminate manner is carried through into a torpid Latin which falls on wholly deaf ears, so that the two old men have no recourse but to wait upon the tramp: "Wither with tremulous and courtly deference, Frost with the deft, noiseless movements of a trained servant". The parallel scene is one of fierce and dangerous confrontation. Ransom's grave Latin leads to an ordeal by riddle. The three questions that Merlin puts effortlessly bridge the Fifth Century and the Twentieth. All ambiguity is ruthlessly set aside, and with the last question all doubt is resolved, for hitherto no one had known the answer but Merlin himself: "Who shall be Pendragon in the time when Saturn descends from his sphere? In what world did he learn war?" Ransom's answer brings an end of all questioning. Merlin submits: "Slowly, ponderously, yet not awkwardly, as though a mountain sank like a wave, he sank on one knee." Even so, others of Ransom's company are not assured, and in this Lewis can mark well the distance between Merlin Ambrosius and Ransom on the one side, and on the other Ransom's own twentieth-century followers.

Merlin has no trace of modern humanitarianism, and he remains scornfully unmoved as he rebuts their fears and suspicions. His language is not the grammar-school language of which Jane has a smattering: it is "the Latin of a man to whom Apuleius and Martianus Capella were the primary classics and whose elegances resembled those of the *Hisperica Famina*". Merlin, emphatically, is not one to be drawn in: he is there, we may truly say, by appointment—"a member of the Organisation" in Ransom's phrase but most certainly, as Dimble tries to make plain to his wife, not a twentieth-century man. So there is no predictability about how he will serve the cause. Indeed, Dimble ruefully admits, "there's more danger of his being too much use than too little".

Lewis sustains the truly mythic quality, even at this late stage in his story. It remains "A fairy-tale for Grown-Ups" in the persistent sense of Merlin's unalterable difference from the present age. It is, too, the final twist in Lewis's theme of reluctance in the face of Divine purpose that now Merlin must realise that he, too, is brought to bay. As he looks at Ransom with dismay, there slowly returns "that almost animal expression, earthy and healthy and with a glint of half-humorous cunning"—"Well . . . if the Earths are stopped, the fox faces the hounds. But had I known who you were at our first meeting, I think I would have put the sleep on you as I did on your Fool." There is only one reply to that, and it preserves the balance of incalculability: "'I am a very light sleeper since I have travelled in the Heavens', said Ransom."

The *dénouement* of the novel, and the climax of the trilogy, finds no favour even with friends and critics as close to Lewis as Owen Barfield and Austin Farrer. For Barfield it is to be linked with Weston's and Devine's humiliation before Oyarsa as evidencing "a certain psychic or spiritual immaturity"; and for Farrer, unless I am mistaken, it prompts the question, "Lewis wrote fairy tales but surely he did not believe them". I pass over the question of what Lewis would have made of the word "believe" in the spirited rebuttal that could certainly be expected of him. Yes, he did believe, for his imagination, he held, had been "baptised". The *opéra-bouffe*, as Barfield not inappropriately terms it, of the Banquet at Belbury, is to my mind Lewis at his best.

We start with the ironic description of the setting—first, "the placid faces of elderly *bons viveurs* whom food and wine had placed in a contentment which no amount of speeches could violate". Things begin to fall apart with deceptive gentleness—at first, single errors of speech, malapropisms that begin to unsettle even Wither—who notices that the company is "attending too much, always a bad sign". The growing "doom of gibberish", a new curse of Babel, gives way to the liberation of the captive beasts of Belbury; and this is the evidence, fatal to the dark masters of the NICE, that "powers more than human had come down to destroy Belbury". Wither himself is brought to book—but not by any stage fire remotely resembling the ending of *Dr. Faustus*. Wither approaching his end remains merely and utterly lethargic. There is a penetrating analysis of that eventual state of mind in which not "even the imminence of his own ruin" can wake a man who, over the long years, has steadily entertained a "repugnance to realities" which has "deepened and darkened, year after year, into a fixed refusal of everything that was in any degree other than himself". Wither has drifted throughout his life: now he drifts into a final abomination. Straik and Witner decapitate Filostrato, and then turn upon each other. Mr. Bultitude the bear settles Wither; Frost immolates himself; he, at the end, "half saw: he wholly hated". Except for Feverstone, speeding away from Belbury, the company of Ransom's enemies is entirely destroyed: and he, sophisticated advocate of the monstrous Institute, is in the end suffocated by its landslide into ruin. Yet we close not with the overthrow of Belbury, but with the onset of Venus; and with the assertion of Logres and an unbroken succession of Pendragons, reaching from "Arthur and Uther and Cassibelaun" to Ransom, seventy-ninth in the great line.

So all falls into place. Mark is brought to a new union with Jane, and Venus reigns for a brief hour as Ransom, his work done, is finally withdrawn. Yet we are not without the reminder that even this epochal victory is no more than an interlude. The ineffable Curry ("so used to superintending the lives of his colleagues that it comes naturally to him to superintend their deaths") is full of plans for the second foundation of Bracton—with himself, naturally, in the leading role.

In this uproarious climax, some readers, I suppose, will respond to Mrs. Dimble's mild conjecture: "Aren't Merlin and the eldils a trifle . . . well, *wholesale?*" The scenes of violent death and disorder complete the *opéra-bouffe* of the banquet: and they in turn are succeeded by the plunging animality of the brute creation. Are these last scenes, in MacPhee's phrase, "indecent"? Some may not find it easy to accept Ransom's assurance: "On the contrary . . . decent, in the old sense, *decens*, fitting, is just what it is. Venus herself is over St. Anne's". Dimble's Shakespearian quotation, "She comes more near the Earth than she was wont . . . to make men mad" is turned another way up: "She comes more near the Earth than she was wont, to—to make Earth sane." Perelandra—the planet to which Ransom had gone, with an entire reluctance, only to end as its liberator—is all about us in the last scene of all, when, manifestly, "Man is no longer isolated. We are now as we ought to be—between the angels who are our elder brothers and the beasts who are our jesters, servants and playfellows."

It is this, I think, that transcends unease. Lewis's imagination embraces the whole of the created Universe as it has been revealed in Ransom's voyagings. Throughout, there has been an undeviating insistence on the moral issues—and, at that, unmistakably, in their simplest form, "the bare willing of obedience". We have seen the part played by reluctance—all the human agents for good have been drawn in against their will, unready to act until, as it seems, the decision is made for them. This has been true not only of the leader, Ransom. It applies, too, to his chief helper at the last hour—a Merlin whom we see finally caught, unawares, in the service of Logres. The counterpart to this unwillingness is the willing surrender— in their appropriate degrees—of the agents of evil: in the highest (or, if we will, the lowest), Wither and Frost; to a lesser extent Feverstone who, characteristically, "knew about the Macrobes, but it wasn't the sort of thing he was interested in"; and to the smaller fry, Cosser and Steele—even Sid and Len, the van drivers who capture Mr. Bultitude. All are part of a sell-out to the Dark Powers, all move in the same orbit which includes even poor Churchwood in his otherwise endearing inconsistency ("all his lectures were devoted to proving the impossibility of ethics, though in private life he walked ten miles rather leave a penny debt unpaid"). We see that there wasn't "a single doctrine practised at Belbury which hadn't been preached by some lecturer at Edgestow". The central lesson is that, on every level, "Those who call for Nonsense will find that it comes". The key to this wholeness of imagining in Lewis—very far, I think, from any "psychic or spiritual immaturity", any tendency, *pace* Farrer, *not* to believe in his own fairy-tales, is to be found in that great concluding passage of *The Allegory of Love* where Lewis speaks of "the complete integration, the harmony, of Spenser's mind": "His work is a growing thing, like a tree; like the world-ashtree itself, with branches reaching to heaven and roots to hell. It reaches up to the songs of angels or the vision of the New Jerusalem and admits among its shining ones the veiled images of God Himself: it reaches down to the horror of fertile chaos beneath the Garden of Adonis and to the grotesque satyrs who protect Una or debauch Hellenore with equal truth to their nature. And between these two extremes comes all the multiplicity of human life . . ."

There, I believe, we have a full answer to any charge of immaturity. Lewis's is truly a wholeness of imagining. In his own sphere, and in his own distinctive way, he attempts a wholeness of truth-telling. If this is what Kathleen Raine has called "a boyish greatness", it is a greatness none the less, deserving in its own measure the praise Lewis accorded to Spenser—*Vitae imaginem expressit.* Lewis's image of life is never at variance with an ironic fidelity to fact, always responsive to the moral obligation which we would gladly set aside if only we could. He deploys a formidable battery of authorial skills, resting with untroubled assurance on what is best characterised by one of his masters, George MacDonald, as "the quiet fullness of ordinary life". There is no psychic or spiritual immaturity. Rather, if we put his work to the test of a fully attentive reading we may record of Lewis, as he did of Spenser, that "to read him is to grow in mental health". Certainly, the space-trilogy comes to rest in the prospect of life awaiting renewal. Jane Studdock crosses a new threshold with the most prosaic of realisations: "Obviously it was high time she went in."

5

Myth and Magic

EWIS HAS LEFT IT ON RECORD that his planetary romances had been "not so much the gratification of . . . fierce curiosity as its exorcism". If we turn back to *The Pilgrim's Regress* we shall be reminded that the triple pillars of his world were Christianity, Reason, and Romanticism. His own enthusiastic reading of medieval literature led him to ascribe to John Gower the qualities he most admired in human nature: "The heart is insular and romantic, the head cool and continental: it is a good combination." One does not have to accept this view of the *Confessio Amantis* to warm to a stirring rehabilitation—Lewis at his best, energetic, charitable, superbly the advocate. As we have seen, Lewis's interplanetary romances written in the 1930s and 1940s dealt with possibilities so remote, at that time, from actuality that there was an ample field for sustained imagination. Spenser's confidence seemed to be vindicated; a boundless prospect lay in view:

> *What if within the Moones faire shining spheare*
> *What if in every other starre unseene*

Of other worldes he happily should heare?
He wonder would much more . . .

But once space-flight had become not only a practical possibility but an established fact, the appeal of "romance" must shift its ground. We turn from "other worldes" to the land of Narnia, which can be entered only by magic, for not only does it exist in a different dimension of time, but it is a world to be entered not arbitrarily, but in its hours of need. A grave wrong is to be righted, an impending total disaster must be averted; and this can be done only by the innocent who are to be brought to a trial which remains unambiguously moral. In the phrase of Seneca that could be said to be a watchword with Lewis, *Nobis quoque militandum*: those who are summoned to this new region will have a fight on their hands. In these terms, the first and oldest of tests is once again to be applied, an ancient story of the utmost gravity to be re-enacted with great simplicity and an abundance of invention. "Romantic theology", Lewis had once before told us, "does not mean being romantic about theology but, rather, being theological about romance." The romances of Narnia take up the powers we have already seen in the space-trilogy—the capacity for extended exposition, penetrating in its simplicity; the satiric insight that enlivens the narrative and can broaden into outright fun; and the warmth of natural observation that can now have free play in the lives of animals, magicians, and wizards, no less than young mortals.

I am perhaps the last man who should take up this theme, for when *The Lion, The Witch and the Wardrobe* first appeared I told the author that he had committed two cardinal errors in children's storytelling—he had encouraged curiosity about the inside of closed spaces (with the obvious risk of the adventurous child finding itself locked in the nearest wardrobe); and he had created an uncomfortably "pi" atmosphere about his supernatural hero, Aslan. To this he retorted equably that, on the first count, young readers had been warned that it was not an example to be followed, and, on the second, that children liked an uncompromising good. Well, perhaps it is never possible to be wholly at ease with any fictional expression of Divine benevolence; but the Wardrobe has been made more acceptable by the explanation of its origin given at the close of *The Magician's Nephew*. I quote the passage at length, for in its relaxed manner it has a freedom and ease which mark a real advance.

The tree from which the wardrobe was made, the narrator explains, had a remarkable origin. But, growing, as it did,

> in the soil of our world, far out of the sound of Aslan's voice and far from the young air of Narnia, it did not bear apples that would revive a dying woman as Digory's Mother had been revived, though it did bear apples more beautiful than any others in England, and they were extremely good for you, though not fully magical. But inside itself, in the very sap of it, the tree so to speak never forgot that other tree in Narnia to which it belonged. Sometimes it would move mysteriously when there was no wind blowing: I think that when this happened there were high winds in Narnia and the English tree quivered because, at that moment, the Narnian tree was rocking and swaying in a strong south-western gale.

There, we may say, imagination deepens into myth, to use that term in the sense Lewis gave to it. Myth, he wrote, offers a rare satisfaction—a pleasure which "depends hardly at all on such usual narrative attractions as suspense or surprise.

Even at a first hearing it is felt to be inevitable." The inevitability is strengthened when we find that the tree, chopped down and carpentered, retains a sleeping magic. It was not to be Digory who discovered the properties of the wardrobe: "someone else did"— and that "was the beginning of all the comings and goings between Narnia and our world". So let us submit with a good will and see something of these comings and goings.

The Magician's Nephew, designed to head the series, proposes nothing less than a Creation and, of course, a Temptation. There is a new perspective on "space-travelling" when the disreputable Uncle Andrew, who here is a sort of Wither/Feverstone—true exemplars, in Lewisian terms, of that Bacon whose interest in magic was plain self-interest—explains what is meant by "another world": "I don't mean another planet, you know; they're part of our world and you could get to them if you went far enough—but a really Other World—another Nature—another universe—somewhere you would never reach even if you travelled through the space of this universe for ever and ever—a world that could be reached only by Magic . . ." There is the farewell to space-fantasy, couched in terms that draw upon the older meaning of the word "world". Any of Lewis's tutorial pupils will recall his reminder that when Satan in *Paradise Lost* alights upon the bare convex of "this world's outermost Orb" he is very, very far from Earth. To see our planet Satan must look through what Lewis called "the manhole"—and there, almost infinitely remote, far, far at the end of the sight-line, is the planet Satan must reach.

So, for Narnian adventure the reader must travel not in space but time, and, at that, a time-dimension which will occasion frequent reminders of its difference from earthly time— as though (to recall Boethius once again) the true liberation

of the human spirit is a release from the order of merely successive time to a simultaneity which knows nothing of past
or future, the terms habitual to us. This has, not surprisingly,
an entirely liberating effect on the writer's imagination. On
the one hand, Narnian lands can grow old, or they can be seen
in their first newness—or, most poignantly, poised at times of
crisis when all stands in balance. Equally, when occasion calls,
continuing earth-time can be made vivid to the reader. That
is why Uncle Andrew is a shabby but would-be dandy of the
Edwardian era, a veritable swell, whose response to his strange
visitant from another world is that of a faded man of what we
are pleased to call "*the* world". Uncle Andrew begins to be
"silly in a very-grown-up way", and there is a Swiftian observation at work when his rather desperate pretensions to gen-
tility are shown—"Not exactly royal, Ma'am"; above all, in his
servile acceptance of the role the Witch in all her scorn as-
signs him: "a little, peddling Magician who works by rules and
books. There is no real Magic in your blood and heart. Your
kind was made an end of in my world a thousand years ago.
But here I shall allow you to be my servant." This devastating broadside leaves Uncle Andrew unscathed, much as Gulliver
had been unmoved by the King of Brobdingnag's savage
characterisation of mankind as the "most pernicious race of
little odious vermin that nature ever suffered to crawl upon
the surface of the earth". Gulliver had attributed this outburst
to "the miserable effects of a confined education". For Uncle
Andrew the Witch is a "fine woman", in Edwardian terms a
"charmer". Affectation, we see, is wholly immune to any sense
of real danger.

　　To be quite truthful, Lewis to my taste rather overdoes the
caricature of would-be worldliness. I could do without the
somewhat laboured detail of Uncle Andrew preparing for his

evening out (the scent on the handkerchief, the "eyeglass, with the thick black ribbon", and so on); and I would be spared the imitation of Edwardian fashionable accent—"Gel", we are knowingly told, "was the way he pronounced girl". Above all, I would willingly dispense with "dem fine woman" which comes in again to mar the last line of all. Lewis perhaps is hoist with his own petard. Here is that over-suspicion of affectation which once led him to condemn as shabby genteel Dryden's

> *Enter, my noble guests, and you shall find*
> *If not a costly welcome yet a kind.*

I do not doubt that in the background lurks poor Pogo, who was young Lewis's first exemplar of The World, in the theological sense of that term: "Pogo was a very minor edition of a Saki, perhaps even a Wodehouse, hero. Pogo was a wit, Pogo was a dressy man, Pogo was a man about town. Pogo was even a lad." Lewis's contempt for this is perhaps over-sharp; but, to be fair, it went with a degree of severity towards himself "a lout of an overgrown fourteen-year-old with a shilling a week pocket money". But, as in *Surprised by Joy*, from which I have been quoting, so here, a pleasant humour is inseparable from any glimpse of Edwardian life. The little housemaid is enraptured throughout the high comedy of Uncle Andrew's intended departure with the Witch-Empress Jadis; for this little observer it makes "a beautifully exciting morning". So, too, with the Cabman who keeps his head; in him there lives the honest man who maintains "there ain't nothing to be afraid of if a chap's led a decent life". One point of his origin in Lewis's experience is unmistakable when, like Paxford, the gardener at The Kilns, the Cabman roundly declares "If you ask me, I think the best thing we could do to pass the time would be to sing a 'ymn".

Lewis's ironic acceptance that the unpretentious does not come without an admixture of the comic is perhaps the other side of what I may call the Uncle Andrew coin. Assuredly, Lewis finds it hard to let go of the social satire. The Wither-like, aldermanic flatulence of Uncle Andrew's eventual terms of reproof to the Witch, when temper gets the better of his fears, swings to the gratuitous side when the indignity of pawning watch and chain is compounded in an impassioned parenthesis: "and let me tell you, Ma'am, that none of our family have been in the habit of frequenting pawnshops, except my cousin Edward, and he was in the Yeomanry". (A last, gentle sally at poor Wallie, Lewis's fellow-soldier, a butt for any criticism of the Yeomanry, which he knew to be the very pink of the military, "having learned it from an Uncle . . . But he could not get it out . . .") These touches are counter-balanced by an unwavering sense that incomprehension can meet only its appropriate reward. Uncle Andrew will make a reasonably good end (in the close, "a nicer and less selfish old man than he had ever been before")—but not until a kind of buffoonery in its own way similar to his own has been practised upon him. The animals, of their courtesy, create a zoo in which old "Brandy", as they innocently call him, must endure captivity. There is the beginning, in all this, of his coming to terms with what he can grasp of his situation (on the animals' lavish gifts "he did fairly well for supper; but it wouldn't be true to say that he passed an agreeable night"). The point is deepened when Aslan replies to Polly's request that something might be done "to unfrighten him". Uncle Andrew, says Aslan, "has made himself unable to hear my voice". He will be given "the only gift he is still able to receive"; and the gift is sleep—a separation "for some few hours from all the torments" he has "devised" for himself.

There speaks the writer whose moral insight is inseparable from a rueful awareness of human nature. Omnipotence must obey the laws of its own creation, not least in these broadly comic instances. The principle applies, too, on what may be called more exalted levels. The Witch, in the end, truly, "has won her heart's desire; she has unwearying strength and endless days like a goddess . . . But length of days with an evil heart is only length of misery and already she begins to know it. All get what they want: they do not always like it." The tone is Johnsonian, the temper that of *Rasselas*. But if there can be no false mercy there can yet be true magic. Digory's deepest wish is granted. The Apple of Youth restores his mother to health, against all ordinary possibility. "It is", says the Doctor, "—it is like a miracle." Perhaps few will read these lines without thinking of Lewis's hope that his wife had been granted a miraculous healing; certainly, no one will wish to dwell on the sadness of the eventual realisation that it was not to be. But the unity of the writer's imagination remains, the foundation alike of satiric vigilance and exalted tenderness.

The Horse and His Boy is altogether freer in aim and execution. There is, indeed, a vein of absurdity, a kind of Irishness of genial poker-faced exaggeration, in the mock quotations from "the poets" of which the boy Shasta's foster-father is fond: "Application to business is the root of prosperity, but those who ask questions that do not concern them are steering the ship of folly towards the rock of indigence." This is a wit which plays around pomposity of speech, and it sits well on Tarkheena Aravis, who, telling her story of escape from enforced marriage to the Grand Vizier, wins the admiration of the nobly-born horse, Bree, overbearing even the main participant's objection: "'I didn't say it half so well at that', muttered the mare. 'Hush, ma'am, hush', said Bree, who was thoroughly enjoying the story. 'She's telling it in the grand Calormene manner and no story-teller in a Tisroc's court could do it better. Pray go on, Tarkheena'." There is more than one reminder of *Rasselas* in reading this version of an "oriental" tale—the ironic asides, the unsleeping sense of the realities of life and the unsparing ridicule of pretence. The memory of school-life in *Surprised by Joy* comes alive in the picture of Tashbaan traffic-laws—or rather, the one (and only) traffic requirement, "which is that everyone who is less important has to get out of the way for everyone who is more important, unless you want a cut from a whip or a punch from the butt end of a spear".

I suppose some readers (though perhaps not many of them children) will find Lewis's sharp sense of physical correction intrusive. It is there not only in incidental touches—and, of course, in the detail of head-slashing, blood-gushing physical combat—but also in a sturdy determination that opponents shall be grotesquely humiliated. Poor Uncle Andrew had to be planted in the ground (and he was lucky not to be upended in the process); now cruel Rabadash has to be suspended from the castle wall—but only two feet from the ground—and then transformed into a donkey, doomed to undergo a final abasement when he must stand before the altar of Tash in the sight of his assembled people. In all this, to be sure, we meet the Lewis who believed with Thomas More (and with Martin Luther) that the devil is a proud spirit who cannot endure to be mocked. And it is of course the energising force of *The Screwtape Letters*, right down to the schoolboy derision of naming the proud if lesser spirits Slubgob, Toadpipe, and so on.

Nothing in this is, in Lewis's terms, accidental, much less merely gratuitous. As Lucy had pleaded for Uncle Andrew, only to be told that he could not be unmade, so now King Lune ("the kindest-hearted of men") has pity on his former opponent, whose sad state is, he says truly, "none of our doing". But discomfiture will not be spared; Rabadash the Ridiculous is the name that must go down to history; and the wisdom of Aslan, in confining Rabadash to a limit of ten miles distance becomes one more instance of the *felix peccatum Adae*. There can be no scope for foreign war where a monarch unable to lead in battle dare not encourage his subordinates to gain glory in his absence.

With Lewis, as always, we are in for the full rigour of the game. Even in this agreeable story with its genuine excitements and delightful exchanges—how deliciously Lasaraleen is cast, a friend whom Aravis finds it hard, even among the most pressing dangers, to keep to the point!—we must none the less have a Doubting Thomas to whom a Risen Lord appears: "Nearer still, my son. Do not dare not to dare. Touch me. Smell me . . ." Perhaps one approach to this, both for those who are moved by it and those who may be offended, is to think of Lewis as a writer for whom all stories of any moment bear upon and find their place in the central Christian story. So, in *Prince Caspian*, pagan exultation is re-animated into Bacchic rout, a company romping pell-mell, and on the verge of overbalancing the continuing story, until "all of a sudden everyone felt at the same moment that the game (whatever it was), and the feast, ought to be over . . ." We touch a similarly ancient source when Lucy, standing among mysterious trees, feels "that she had just missed something: as if she had spoken to the trees a split second too soon or a split second too late, or used all the right words except one, or put in one word that was just wrong".

One recalls Lewis's reverence for paganism—for example,

philosophically, for that *praeparatio evangelica* which he saw as "inherent in much immediately sub-Christian experience"; or, critically, in his response to the invocation that opens Book III of Milton's *Paradise Lost*, when the poet, calling upon the almost inexpressible—"Hail holy Light, offspring of Heav'n first-born"—draws upon the ancient practice of getting in the right name for the god invoked, lest the spell fail. In this way, Milton subtly unites the nearly unimaginable attributes of Christian Deity with the many names ventured upon by timorous but urgent petitioners down through the ages—a sensitive reading that does not fail to delight in the dexterity by which the transition is made—"Or hear'st thou rather"—resembling the stylised art of the dancer, changing step with a reversal of initial metric thrust. More widely, it is that impulse towards final order—"a place for everything and everything in its place"—that led Lewis to maintain with entire conviction that Christianity is a school in which all previous experience can be put to good use. The Bacchic rout, the glorious romp of Caspian's Narnia restored, stops short of the destructiveness of the Banquet at Belbury; but each is a response to the inclusiveness of Lewis's understanding of God's ways with mankind.

This coexists, of course, with a lively sense of actuality. The version of MacPhee who comes to the fore in the tale of *Prince Caspian* is an enduring witness to Lewis's sense that Faith is, above all else, a virtue; sometimes, he readily confessed, the Christian scheme of things looked very odd to the rationalist in him. Hence the insistence upon a capacity for mere obedience. Trumpkin may not believe in the wonder-working properties of the Horn—"But what's that got to do with it? I might as well die on a wild goose chase as die here. You are my King. I know the difference between giving ad-

vice and taking orders." That "bare willing of obedience" is
an abiding principle throughout the *Chronicles of Narnia*; and
since it is so, allowing no variation or exception, there is ample
room for banter, for cheerful parody, and for a kind of Malorian
Wardour Street language which has its own capacity for self-
parody. So, when Peter dictates his challenge to Miraz we start
with measured terms of passable heroic: "*For to prevent the
effusion of blood, and for the avoiding all other inconveniences
likely to grow from the wars now levied in our realm of Narnia
. . .*" But when we come to "*the most abhominable, bloody, and
unnatural murder . . .*", then Doctor Cornelius must be told—
"abhominable—don't forget to spell it with an н, Doctor—
bloody, and unnatural . . ." It is a cheerful note of mockery
(for a moment reminiscent, for me, of T. H. White), in its own
way a skilful changing of step, a lightness of touch that happily dissolves into absurdity, for it is cousin to a well-founded
seriousness. If nothing is made in vain, then no order of
mimesis is barred.

The *Voyage of the Dawn Treader* can be seen as an extended
instance of the relaxed manner. The dragoning and undra-
goning of Eustace is the farthest reach of severity; though even
there honesty will out: "It would be nice, and fairly nearly true,
to say that 'from that time forth Eustace was a different boy'.
To be strictly accurate, he began to be a different boy. He had
relapses. There were still many days when he could be very
tiresome." Yet the conclusion is genial: "But most of those I
shall not notice. The cure had begun."

Perhaps we should characterise the dominant mood of
Lewis's Narnian writing as a sort of genial severity of the widest
compass, sanctioning outright comedy. There is a vivid reminder of *The Pilgrim's Regress* in the lighthearted treatment
of the Duffers, where dialectical energy turns neat somersaults

of logicality: "The Magician sighed. 'You wouldn't believe the troubles I've had with them. A few months ago they were all for washing up the plates and knives before dinner; they said it saved time afterwards. I've caught them planting boiled potatoes to save cooking them when they were dug up. One day the cat got into the dairy and twenty of them were at work moving all the milk out; no one thought of moving the cat.'" Equally, there is scope for gravely beautiful imaginings. The Sea Girl whom Lucy sees for a moment—"a quiet, lovely-looking girl with a sort of crook in her hand"—owes something to Wordsworth's Highland Reaper. So, too, the dark enchantment which threatens Lord Rhoop in his voyaging draws upon both the *Odyssey* and Coleridge's *Ancient Mariner*; the comfort Reepicheep can give Eustace derives from Boccaccio's *de Casibus Virorum Illustrium*; and so on. All are perfectly in place, borne along on a tide of strong but tranquil imagining; and as the voyage of the *Dawn Treader* draws to a close, the end of habitual reality begins to loom: "Every day and every hour the light became more brilliant and still they could not bear it. No one ate or slept and no one wanted to, but they drew buckets of dazzling water from the sea, stronger than wine and somehow wetter, more liquid, than ordinary water . . ."

"Wetter, more liquid, than ordinary water . . ." We are back with the C. S. Lewis of Gordon's discussion class in Michaelmas 1922, maintaining that Spenser's carpet of grass was greener than grass as we ordinarily know it. He needed, he told Coghill, the Greek word *gános* to express the radiance of a true reality, the Platonic idea of greenness. This heightened awareness, an habitual gravitation towards Final Cause, so far from suppressing or overlaying argumentative vigour and satiric sharpness, is wholly consonant with them. To use one of Lewis's well-worn insistences, Plato's is genuinely a ladder

in which the lower rungs are not cancelled or abandoned when
the ascent is to be made. In *The Voyage of the Dawn Treader*
a final landfall is at hand. The writing in the close has a relaxed energy, a grave simplicity, when the Lamb transformed
into a Lion speaks of the purpose of journeying to Narnia and
the necessity of return—alike for the Pevensie children and
for all Lewis's readers: "This was the very reason why you were
brought to Narnia, that by knowing me here for a little, you
may know me better there."

The Silver Chair, next in the chronicle sequence and the
penultimate adventure, shows Lewis's imagination at its best—
endlessly fertile, mature, humorous, and abounding in lively
touches. It is, I think, to some extent marred by that Wardour
Street virtuosity which had always been somewhat intrusive,
along with the archaic slang of a past era—"By Jove!"; "Faugh!"
But now, unless I am much mistaken, there is some overbal-
ance. "'In a good hour,' cried the Prince; 'Sir, be pleased to
take another breast of pigeon, I entreat you'": and in the mouth
of the Witch: "As for you, my lord Prince, that art a man full
grown, fie upon you!"—a heady mixture altogether, Barfield's
"pure pastiche!". But these are sunspots. The sheer fertility
of imagination is captivating. One thinks of the giants who
"jeered at one another in long, meaningless words of about
twenty syllables each"; the Earthmen who "came all round them
padding on large, soft feet, on which some had ten toes, some
twelve, and others none"; the sturdiness of Puddleglum con-
fronting the Witch—"You may have blotted it out and turned
it dark like this, for all I know ... But I know I was there once";
above all, the fine portrayal of the Dark Knight under enchantment; and, in the close, the Great Snow Dance, perfectly (here,
as it was in the conclusion of *The Problem of Pain*) the para-
digm of freedom in submission to constraint set, forever un-

forgettably, amid moonlight, and that "wild, woodland blood" that dances until break of day. *The Silver Chair* is for me the perfect Narnian story, and it is the better for the light-hearted snook in the end at Experiment House, when (after some expulsions) even the Head's friends "saw that the Head was no use as a Head, so they got her made an Inspector to interfere with other Heads. And when they found she wasn't much good even at that, they got her into Parliament where she lived happily ever after." This can fairly be called Swiftian in its open-eyed candour. *Gulliver's Travels*, we know, suitably expurgated, was banished to the nursery. The *Chronicles of Narnia* have already found their way into grown-up readership. (I had nearly said "adult", before I realised to what sad uses the word has fallen.) But this of course is not in any sense a promotion, an advance into a really understanding readership. Children are likely to remain those most responsive to an unforced fertility of imagination and to a golden seriousness of purpose—unique combination!

With *The Last Battle* the tide turns homeward. But not before the greatest of all disasters impends. We feel again the energy of protest against "Men without chests", as they were called in *The Abolition of Man*, and against that form of devilry which, readily using imposture for its own ends, must find itself, in the long run, in turn used—to its own destruction. But before that, once more the call must go out; once again, battle is to be joined. Aslan manifestly "is not a tame Lion". So the forces of deception plumb a deeper level. How should anyone know what Aslan will do? The King asks the unanswerable question: "'Would it not be better to be dead than to have this horrible fear that Aslan has come and is not like the Aslan we have believed in and longed for? It is as if the sun rose one day and were a black sun.'

"'I know', said Jewel. 'Or as if you drank water and it were *dry* water.'"

Those who read *A Grief Observed* on its first appearance wondered at the supreme honesty with which, in the depth of near-despair, "N.W. Clerk" could face the possibility of final deception: "Talk to me about the truth of religion and I'll listen gladly. Talk to me about the duty of religion and I'll listen submissively. But don't come talking to me about the consolation of religion or I shall suspect that you don't understand." And, deepest of all: "What reason have we, except our own desperate wishes, to believe that God is, by any standard we can conceive, 'good'? Doesn't all the *prima facie* evidence suggest exactly the opposite?" So the darkest hour is upon Narnia when the creatures come to fear that Aslan is "not like the Aslan we have believed in and longed for". Soon it will be proclaimed that "Tash is Aslan: Aslan is Tash". Against this darkest of backgrounds, battle is to be joined, and there is a workmanlike energy in the field-tactics employed against the Calormenes—a shrewd use of enfilading fire that almost succeeds, until enemy reinforcements endlessly at hand make withdrawal the only course. Inevitably, reality narrows to a single point of intensity. The Black Hole of the stable-prison vividly focuses the plight of those who will not accept release, for they cannot believe in the existence of light; and once again Aslan must manifest himself to show "both what I can, and what I cannot do". The miraculous feast that is provided for the Dwarfs is devoured, certainly; but, in accordance with the maxim on which Lewis founded his concept of literary influence, *quicquid recipitur, recipitur ad modum recipientis*: "They thought they were eating and drinking only the sort of things you might find in a stable." So, inevitably "every Dwarf began suspecting that every other Dwarf had found something nicer than he had, and they started grabbing and snatching, and went on to quarrelling" and in the end Aslan must sadly show their "prison is only in their own minds, yet they are in that prison; and so afraid of being taken in that they cannot be taken out".

Aslan, therefore, has "other work to do", and the story leads first to a Judgement Day, and then to a dissolution of the visible world, when vegetation dies, the monsters themselves grow old and perish, the sea rises; and the Timegiant, Chronos himself, takes the Sun in his hand and squeezes it like an orange. This is some of Lewis's best writing in the entire *Chronicles of Narnia*—the activity of a superbly concrete imagination. Nothing here is cloudy or imprecise. In this final hour, Emeth the Calormene re-appears, witness to a cardinal truth, that "a noble friend is the best gift and a noble enemy the next best". ("Opposition", we remember, "is true friendship"—Lewis's special emphasis for the ancient truth, *magis amica veritas*); and nothing remains but to move "further up and further in". The moral principle to which we ascend is one that honours the virtuous pagan, the *Sylvestris*—one who, living apart from the reach of Divine revelation, is yet obedient to the highest moral imperative he knows. Because Tash and Aslan are *not* one but very opposites, Aslan can take to himself the service done to Tash, for "no service which is vile can be done to me, and none which is not vile can be done to him". As throughout, and now finally made plain, "all find what they truly seek". When the last frontier is crossed, the Platonically Real is at hand, and nothing is veritably lost: "All of the old Narnia that mattered, all the dear creatures, have been drawn into the real Narnia through the Door. And of course it is different; as different as a real thing is from a shadow or as waking life is from a dream."

The ending is a grand re-union: "Everyone you had ever heard of (if you knew the history of those countries) seemed to be there." There was "greeting and kissing and hand-shaking and old jokes revived"—for, a characteristic touch, "you've no idea how good an old joke sounds when you take it out again after a rest of five or six hundred years . . ."

There is the defence, if one were wanted, for Lewis as truly *laudator temporis acti*—no "Sectary of Backwardness", as Geoffrey Grigson once unkindly termed him, doomed to live only to decry the present. When dogged resolution to occupy the last ditch on the trench-map is no longer at issue, the author of the *Chronicles of Narnia* can present all things triumphantly gathered to a new beginning. Then it can most truly be said "they all lived happily ever after".

6

Reason and Romanticism

EWIS CONCLUDED his talks on *Christian Behaviour* (1943):
"though Christianity seems at first to be all about morality, all about duties and rules and guilt and virtue,
yet it leads you on, out of all that, into something beyond. One
has a glimpse of a country where they don't talk of those things,
except perhaps as a joke".

In one of his last published works, *Letters to Malcolm*
(1964), he writes of having tried "to make every pleasure into
a channel of adoration": "This heavenly fruit is instantly redo-
lent of the orchard where it grew. This sweet air whispers of
the country from whence it blows . . . To experience the tiny
theophany is itself to adore . . . One's mind runs back up the
sunbeam to the sun."

The Boxen of childhood, we recall, had become a single
state, formed from the union of Animal-land and India. They
remained in the "outer life", along with "much that would
ordinarily be called imagination". But once the juvenile world
of Boxen had been touched with the search for "Joy", then, truly,
the creative mind ran "back up the sunbeam to the sun". Moral

84

awareness is in no sense supplanted. But there can no longer be any room for a merely "prosaic moralism", one "which confines goodness to the region of Law and Duty".

One must often be reminded of Dr. Johnson when opening almost any work by Lewis; and Lewis's admiration for Johnson is well attested. But there remains this great contrast between them. Johnson's temperament remained at odds with the demands of his religion, as he understood that religion. Disputatious, pragmatic, and irremediably melancholic, Johnson embraced the desperate conclusion that we must do what is right because God commands it. So God is the absolute sovereign who will not be gainsaid. Romantic rebellion against this despot, as against all manifestations of arbitrary power, was therefore natural and necessary—for the young Clive Hamilton writing *Spirits in Bondage* (1919) no less than for others. The *nom de guerre*, incidentally, might very easily be penetrated since the volume includes a ten-page list of Heinemann's poetry, on the first page of which "George [*sic*] Lewis, *Spirits in Bondage*" is listed. There follows a brief account of Lieut. G. [*sic*] S. Lewis's education and war-service. (The poetry of "Lieut. Siegfried Sassoon, M C", and of "Captain Robert Graves" is listed on the same page.) It is perhaps curious that Lewis, who was invariably known to his friends as "Jack", should not, in this instance, succeed in establishing either a pseudonym or his true name.

Spirits in Bondage, as I mentioned earlier, is described by its author as "A Cycle of Lyrics" and divides into three parts—"The Prison House; Hesitation; The Escape". The theme is a journey to a land of heart's desire:

> *In my coracle of verses I will sing of lands unknown,*
> *Flying from the scarlet city where a Lord that knows no*
> *pity*

Mocks the broken people praying round his iron throne,
—Sing about the Hidden Country fresh and full of quiet
    green.
Sailing over seas uncharted to a port that none has seen.

For the poet there is a contrast between the landfall he seeks
and the authority of a God who is "very strong", having "the
keys of Hell". Reason justifies man in proud rebellion:

Yet I will not bow down to thee nor love thee,
For looking in my own heart I can prove thee,
And know this frail, bruised being is above thee.

God's power is a lesser thing than man's compassion and search
for understanding:

Our love, our hope, our thirsting for the right,
Our mercy and long seeking of the light,
Shall we change these for thy relentless might?

("Relentless might", it may be noted, is opposed to:

The ancient hope that still will rise again,
Of a just God that cares for earthly pain—

a foreshadowing of *The Problem of Pain*, to appear with the
onset of another World War.)

The second section, "Hesitation", includes some notable
"Aaexandrines" where the image of an empty, silent house—

a house that most of all on earth I hate—

focuses in the climax upon

a little, silent room
Where Someone's always waiting, waiting in the gloom
To draw me with an evil eye, and hold me fast—

and the conclusion is prophetic—

> *Yet thither doom will drive me and He will win at last.*

The conflict leads the poet to envy those who

> *are not fretted with desire,*

for each reverse returns him to himself:

> *Then suddenly again, the room,*
> *Familiar books about me piled,*
> *And I alone amid the gloom,*
> *By one more mocking dream beguiled.*

We may be reminded of "Busirane's appalling house", the "unbearable silent splendour in the House of Busirane", in Lewis's account of *The Faerie Queene* in *The Allegory of Love*; or, in lighter mood, "I am a product of long corridors, empty sunlit rooms, upstairs indoor silences, attics explored in solitude, distant noises of gurgling cisterns and pipes, and the noises of wind under the tiles". But it was, too, in the same "New House" of his boyhood that "the blows of change began to fall", and there, too, in the end, that "all settled happiness, all that was tranquil and reliable, disappeared from my life".

Clive Hamilton, at all events, must know himself

> *still no nearer to the Light,*
> *And still no further from myself,*
> *Alone and lost in clinging night*
> *—(The clock's still ticking on the shelf),*

which poignantly foretells the ending of *The Great Divorce* (1946): "I awoke in a cold room, hunched on the floor beside a black and empty grate, the clock striking three, and the siren howling overhead."

The third and final section, "The Escape", is an escape into intellectual and spiritual endeavour. Oxford is seen as

> *The Spirit's stronghold—barred against despair.*

Man's power knows no limits, if he will but set himself to the task of learning—a truth expressed with Wordsworthian simplicity:

> *We could revel day and night*
> *In all power and all delight*
> *If we learned to think aright.*

The best hope for man is an ultimate escape, in which he will be merged with Life itself:

> *When glory I have built in dreams*
> *Along some fiery sunset gleams,*
> *And my dead sin and foolishness*
> *Grow one with Nature's whole distress,*
> *To perfect being I shall win,*
> *And where I end will Life begin.*

There remains a quest to be pursued; but the last lines in the book place it beyond attainment in this life. The poem is entitled "Death in Battle"—a death which will "Open the gates" of a "Country of Dreams", lying

> *Beyond the tide of the ocean, hidden and sunk away,*
> *Out of the sound of battles, near to the end of day,*
> *Full of dim woods and streams.*

Here, very clearly, there is no reconciliation between "sweet desire" and God's "relentless might". The ending of life may admit man to the happiness he seeks; meanwhile, intellectual endeavour is all.

Lewis's claim that the later book, *The Pilgrim's Regress*, was "written by one who has proved them all [the supposed objects of desire] to be wrong" is clearly justified. What is no less evident is the originality of the *Regress*. For here, to adapt the old saying, Lewis has summoned reason to the aid of imagination. Now "the merely argued dialectic" of his philosophical progress—the transition from "popular realism" to philosophical idealism, thence to pantheism, thence to Theism, and so to Christianity—is seen to converge upon the same goal as "the dialectic of Desire", the refusal of all false objects of that desire. In this light, man is forced "not to propound, but to live through, a sort of ontological proof". Lewis therefore found himself facing two sets of opponents, who while "hostile to one another" were united in their "common enmity to 'immortal longings'". On the one hand were the followers of Freud and D. H. Lawrence; but worse (it "put me out of patience" was Lewis's admission) was an equal and opposite danger, manifest in "the scorn which claimed to be from above, and which was voiced by the American 'Humanists', the Neo-Scholastics, and some who wrote for *The Criterion*".

The road Lewis's pilgrim must walk therefore lies between "foetid swamps" to the South, and "barren, aching rocks" to the North. As for the Northerners, among whom Eliot was plainly, at that time, to be included, Lewis's conviction was that such people were "condemning what they did not understand". If romanticism were for the Northerners "spilled religion", Lewis would reply that "those bright drops on the floor" might be for a man "the beginning of a trail which, duly followed, will lead him in the end to taste the cup itself". For some men, he added, no other trail might be possible.

Lewis here speaks of a truth proved upon his own pulses. In *Surprised by Joy* (1955)—sub-titled, it is well to remember,

"The Shape of my Early Life"—the desire, "Joy" itself, is the dominant theme, transcending the intellectual progress. But now there is no search for a land beyond the setting sun: "when the great moments came I did not break away from the woods and cottages that I read of to seek some bodiless light shining beyond them, but gradually, with a swelling continuity (like the sun at mid-morning burning through a fog) I found the light shining on those woods and cottages, and then on my own past life, and on the quiet room where I sat and on my old teacher where he nodded above his little Tacitus". Here is the distinctive break with both an anxiously rigorous moralism and an agonised romanticism: "Up till now each visitation of Joy had left the common world momentarily a desert—'The first touch of the earth went nigh to kill'. Even when real clouds or trees had been the material of the vision, they had been so only by reminding me of another world; and I did not like the return to ours."

A journey homeward to habitual self is the ending which both the moralist and the rebellious romantic have good cause to fear. For Lewis, on first reading MacDonald's *Phantastes*, the quarrel was momentarily made up: "now I saw the bright shadow coming out of the book into the real world and resting there, transforming all common things and yet itself unchanged. Or, more accurately, I saw the common things drawn into the bright shadow. *Unde hoc mihi?*" As Lewis wrote elsewhere, "I should have been shocked in my 'teens if anyone had told me that what I learned to love in *Phantastes* was goodness". He continued: "But now that I know, I see there was no deception. The deception is all the other way round—in that prosaic moralism which confines goodness to the region of Law and Duty, which never lets us feel in our face the sweet air blowing from 'The land of righteousness', never reveals that elusive Form which if once seen must inevitably be desired with all but sensuous desire—the thing (in Sappho's phrase) 'more gold than gold'." Lewis may be described as a "romantic theologian" in the sense which his friend Charles Williams invented for the term—not, as Lewis was careful to point out, "one who is romantic about theology but one who is theological about romance, one who considers the theological implications of those experiences which are called romantic". What Lewis said of Williams may be wholly applied to himself: "The belief that the most serious and ecstatic experiences either of human love or of imaginative literature have such theological implications, and that they can be healthy and fruitful only if the implications are diligently thought out and severely lived, is the root principle of all his work."

Does this equation of sweet desire and moral duty mean that in the end the romantic impulse is thwarted or made negligible? Certainly, the fever of pursuit is ended. When not only imagination but reason had assented to Christian belief, "Joy" became for Lewis much less important in terms of seeking. The pointers remained; but now that the land of heart's desire was known for what it truly was, there was no impulse to "stop and stare . . . 'We would be at Jerusalem.'" To know the destination is of course not to have arrived. But it gave a special sanction to each "tiny theopany" when the mind might run "back up the sunbeam to the sun".

The distance between this and Dr. Johnson's view of imagination could hardly be greater. Chapter XLIII of *Rasselas* is uncompromisingly headed "The dangerous prevalence of imagination": "In time some particular train of ideas fixes the attention, all other intellectual gratifications are rejected, the mind, in weariness or leisure, recurs constantly to the favourite conception, and feasts on the luscious falsehood whenever she is offended with the bitterness of truth." For Johnson, danger is paramount: what begins as diversion must end in servitude: "By degrees the reign of fancy is confirmed; she grows first imperious, and in time despotick. Then fictions begin to operate as realities, false opinions fasten upon the mind, and life passes in dreams of rapture or of anguish." It is against this background that we move to the next chapter of *Rasselas*, to discourse with an old man "whose years have calmed his passions, but not clouded his reason"—an old man whose wisdom, sadly, is inaccessible to the young. "Joy" is very far off. Johnson, we may recall, once qualified his praise of a sermon by Blair in these terms: "There is one part of it which I disapprove . . . which is, that 'he who does not feel joy in religion is far from the kingdom of heaven!' There are many good men whose fear of God predominates over their love. It may discourage. It was rashly said."

It is from this point of view a question properly to be asked, as B. H. Bronson once asked, "whether his religion did not bring him more continuous disquiet than it ever brought comfort, till the very end". Bronson went on to observe that Johnson's reasons for belief "are rooted in distress and misery, and they come from him without qualification or mitigation": "None would have recourse to an invisible power, but that all other subjects have eluded their hopes." (*Idler*, No.89)

We return then to the shadow cast by the lawgiver, an absolute Sovereign. Rebellion against this Despot, as against all lesser manifestations of arbitrary power, is seen to be natural and necessary. D. G. James, in a wholly original treatment (*The Romantic Comedy*, 1948), once discussed two nineteenth-century acceptances of Christianity—in Coleridge and in Newman. Different as are their final positions, in neither was the long quarrel between reason and romanticism made up; and this is perhaps the central reason why a penitential sadness, "a certain awful wistfulness, a frost 'deep almost as life'" inheres in "the very wisdom and humility of these men". Newman, as James points out, was to say of himself that "his soul resembled glass in transmitting the warmth of faith to others, itself remaining cold". Painfully and lastingly missing is any fusion between religious belief and romantic insight.

When that fusion is made, in terms of "joy" or "desire", we notice two characteristics. First, for Lewis, as for the major romantics, "no pleasure would be too ordinary or too usual for such reception", "from the first taste of the air when I look out of the window—one's whole cheek becomes a sort of palate—down to one's soft slippers at bedtime". Second, for Lewis as opposed to Johnson, no final distinction can be made between the merely sensuous and the aesthetic. All "pleasure" is now one subject: there is no final separation of "desires distinct from sense". For Lewis as for Johnson (both well aware "there is no man ... who can regulate his attention wholly by his will"), a discipline is to be observed—but now it is seen precisely as disciplined attention to our pleasures.

The argument is noteworthy. We start with the well-recognised truth that patience in adversity is required of the Christian. For Johnson, indeed, it was the supreme truth of experience: "Philosophy may infuse stubbornness, but Religion only can give patience." Lewis could count on Johnson's wholehearted agreement so far: "William Law remarks that people are merely 'amusing themselves' by asking for the patience which a famine or a persecution would call for if, in the meantime, the weather and every other inconvenience sets them grumbling. One must learn to walk before one can run." But this is seen as exactly one half of a complex truth. Patience is not all that is enjoined upon man. He is to adore as well as obey: "We—or at least I—shall not be able to adore God on the highest occasions if we have learned no habit of doing so on the lowest. At best, our faith and reason will tell us that He is adorable, but we shall not have *found* Him so, not have 'tasted and seen'." Johnson (in a notable *Adventurer* essay, No. 108) had perceived the same truth but only in the sphere of conduct: "It is not only uncertain, whether, through all the casualties and dangers which beset the life of man, we shall be able to reach the time appointed for happiness or wisdom; but it is likely, that whatever now hinders us from doing that which our reason and conscience declare necessary to be done, will equally obstruct us in times to come."

Lewis's is the recovery of a central tradition of Christian thought in which reason is paramount. "They err", said Hooker, "who think that of the will of God to do this or that there is no reason besides His will." On this view, the rightness, the inherent rationality, of the Divine will is apparent to all men, Christian and pagan alike: and freedom to conform to or depart from that will is their inalienable right. More, if reason is paramount, it is comprehensive. The "right reason" (or "practical reason") which rules in the sphere of conduct is not other than a rightness of response to the created world, a delighted recognition that though man is a stranger here, his home is prepared for him. Home-sickness is only felt as a desperate condition if there is no ground for supposing that there is a home.

In the nineteenth century former rebels, Coleridge and Newman outstanding among them, embrace authoritative story as revealed religion. But if I am right it is not until the middle twentieth century that a working reconciliation is offered not simply between mythology and Christian story, nor merely between the ethics of duty—"the bare willing of obedience"—

and the ethics of virtue, but between reason (mistakenly thought to be the enemy of both romanticism and revealed religion) and the nature of intense awareness—when that awareness is understood neither as idle delusion nor (the romantic illusion) as the sole entry upon ultimate reality, but as pleasure, inseparable from the whole range of pleasurable experience but calling for and rewarding disciplined attention.

7

The Writer as Scholar

"YOU MAY MAKE A WRITER or a scholar of him, but you'll not make anything else. You may make up your mind to *that*." Thus Kirk to Lewis *père*. The reader will have noticed that in dealing with Lewis's fictional writings I have more than once resorted to his scholarly work for close comparison—most often, for an alternative rendering of the same theme. I shall hope to show that the fundamental impulse in the scholarly work is at one with what we respond to in the fictional works—an energy which combines in unique fashion creative imagination and ratiocinative ardour. Lewis heightens sensibility as he challenges torpor.

I begin with a certain wariness, evident in Lewis's earlier scholarly writings and never entirely lost—an unsleeping sense of practical relevance. What is the worth of scholarly work unless it can be shown to bear on modern values? So, in a note which appeared in *The Review of English Studies* as early as 1933, Lewis apologised for setting out certain *minutiae* of change in the text of Milton's *Comus*. Whatever may be thought of Milton's judgement in making the changes, they offer, he said,

an instructive example of "what may be called poetic chas-
tity": and this is contrary to what may please modern taste—
"Not so would Donne or D. H. Lawrence have chosen". The
mention of Donne points forward to Lewis's essay on Donne's
love-poetry contributed to the Grierson *Festschrift* (1938), with
its damning verdict: "Donne's real limitation is not that he
writes *about*, but that he writes *in*, a chaos of violent and contradictory passions." Supposing we give one twist to the ka-
leidoscope, we could have: "Donne's real achievement is to give
the illusion that he writes not about but *in* a chaos of violent
and contradictory passions"—in other words, that Donne re-
invested the lyric with the authority of drama. But this is not
a perspective that Lewis will allow; and perhaps we begin to
sense the *cordon sanitaire* implicit in Lewis's "Personal Heresy". If merely biographical facts are to be kept at a remove
from the work, then the work itself may be placed in the same
forbidden zone if it is highly subjective—or appears to be so.
I suspect the cause of this aversion lies in that willed dismissal
of the self which Barfield outlines so well: "Self-knowledge, for
him, had come to mean recognition of his own weaknesses
and shortcomings and nothing more. Anything beyond that
he sharply suspected, both in himself and in others, as a symp-
tom of spiritual megalomania." This is, I do not doubt, something of a limitation in the critic of historical literature, to
which I now turn.

I begin with *The Allegory of Love* which, appearing in 1936,
won Lewis high praise from many quarters. It is a work which
has all the authority of a mind of the highest quality marking out clear paths in a complex and absorbing mass of material. As such it effortlessly joins company with that very small
class of books for which a future can be confidently predicted.
They are those works which handle a large subject—large not

in range, merely, but in significance to the human spirit—with a pioneer's skill, marking out new country and leaving an indelible impression for all subsequent settlement of the area. They can be wrongheaded in approach or mistaken in detail; but they must be not so much accounts of literature in the past as themselves instances of literature in being. When Anatole France spoke of literary criticism as recording the adventures of the soul among masterpieces he doubtless had something of the sort in mind. Alas! from the ordinary output of criticism we can only conclude that there are some very dull souls about. Yet there is a rare category of works of criticism that justifies the aphorism. One thinks of Bradley's *Shakespearian Tragedy*, Ker's *Epic and Romance*, John Livingston Lowes's *Road to Xanadu*, to name no others. Each is a book which not only shows great powers of penetration and organising skill; each succeeds in communicating the activity of a mind of the highest quality entirely intent on the material before it, to which it is giving new and distinctive shape. Let us describe these books in one word: they are all in the highest degree *readable*.

Lewis's *The Allegory of Love* surely belongs in any such classification. There is a luminous intelligence of the first order at work—an angel who writes as only Lewis could, humorously, graphically, and with an exalted seriousness. To be sure, there are things to be disputed, in Lewis's book as in all the others of its distinguished class. Lewis was the first to point them out. On a Collection paper in which I had adopted, too uncritically for him, his view of the medieval antithesis between love and marriage, he himself wrote in parody of me, "Mr. Lewis seems to forget that Palamon and Arcite both wanted to marry Emelye." But, as with the other works I have listed, here is a *book*, obedient to the first rule of writing—that on every page it asks to be read. How many extended works of literary criticism are truly unputdownable? It is the severest test; and *The Allegory of Love* triumphantly survives it.

Even here, we meet an ambiguity in the title itself—by now, no doubt, so well established that we pass it over without thought. But does the allegory of love mean a treatment of the love-allegory (a literary form), or does it indicate that the passion of love is itself "allegorical"? Lewis's own original title, *The Allegorical Love Poem*, was clear enough. But it appears that the Oxford University Press thought "the word 'allegorical'—though not 'allegory'—tended to put people off". One of Lewis's suggestions for an alternative was truly a writer's choice, *The House of Busirane*. But the formulation, *The Allegory of Love*, prevailed—with the important sub-title, "A Study in Medieval Tradition", and Lewis's sustaining creed enshrined in the quotation from Horace placed firmly on the title-page:

> *Multa renascentur quae jam cecidere, cadentque*
> *Quae nunc sunt in honore.*

This even-handedness of justice leads to spirited rehabilitation (a significant title for a later collection of essays) of the unfashionable. A leading instance is the half-chapter on Gower which is Lewis at his best—positive, affirmative, and genial. We may perhaps cavil at the notion of a fourteenth-century writer as a romantic born before his time; but any reader would be hard-hearted indeed who did not warm to Lewis's stirring restoration-work. Similarly, with the treatment of Chaucer Lewis is thoroughly on form. Wishing to focus on the courtly and erotic he places interest in the narrative art of *The Canterbury Tales* at a suitable distance, and then moves to an exquisite treatment of the *Troilus*, culminating in the treatment of Troilus himself, "a character so easily made happy and so easily broken", one for whom "there can be no tragedy in the Greek or in the modern sense", so that the ending is "pathos pure and unrelieved". The writing in this passage reaches an excellence Lewis never surpassed; and the whole book, conceived and conducted on a level at once exalted and concretely illustrated cannot fail to bowl over any but the most prejudiced reader. From R. W. Chambers, always living in the shade of his great master, W. P. Ker, came the highest tribute: "on second reading it seems to me quite the greatest thing done in England for medieval studies since Ker's *Epic and Romance*". E. M. W. Tillyard's utterance was characteristic: "At last . . . a medievalist who is also a critic." Ifor Evans, reviewing the book for *The Observer*, remarked, "His excellence as a writer lies in the fact that wherever the road turns he is never uncertain of the ultimate direction, and never dull". Evans concluded: "In an age in which scholarship and general literature are wrongly separated this volume is in danger of being set aside. This would be regrettable. No one with an interest in the background of his own mind or a taste for good writing will find it negligible." That strikes the right note. *The Allegory of Love* is, before all else, the work of a writer. Here is a writer who delights in the varied skills of translator—unfailingly lively, and unflinchingly versatile. A hundred examples from all over his published works leap to mind. Among the high-spirited there is the translation of the *Concilium in Monte Romarici* into rhyming couplets:

> The reader of that gospel gay
> Was Sister Eva, who (they say)
> Understands the practick part
> Of the Amatory Art . . .

Or the translation and comment on Prudentius's

> *Os quoque parce*
> *Erigit et comi moderatur gaudia vultu,*

which becomes

> *Uplifts her face*
> *With moderated cheer, and civil looks*
> *Tempering her joy.*

("Nothing", adds Lewis, "could suggest more vividly the smirk of a persevering governess who has finally succeeded in getting a small boy into trouble with his father.") Among the *tours de force* must be placed the translation of two extended passages from Alanus de Insulis into sixteenth-century prose, and a "Middle English" rendering from Chretien's *Lancelot* (both in *The Allegory of Love*); or, even, the style of speech given Merlin in *That Hideous Strength*. The motive in all this was not idle virtuosity. When he came to write his volume in the *Oxford History of English Literature*, Lewis consistently turned his neo-Latin authors into sixteenth-century English—"not simply", as he said, "for the fun of it, but to guard the reader from a false impression he might otherwise receive. When passages from Calvin, Scaliger, or Erasmus in modern English jostle passages from vernacular writers with all the flavour of their period about them, it is fatally easy to get the feeling that the Latinists are somehow more enlightened, less remote, less limited by their age, than those who wrote English. It seemed worth some pains to try to remove so serious and so latent a misconception". If few had been sensitive enough to perceive this defect, inherent in the historical study of literature, even fewer had the wit and scholarship to remedy it.

A writer, again, with a fine sense of climax, as in the treatment of palinode which closes the first chapter, when "We hear the bell clang; and the children, suddenly hushed and grave, and a little frightened, troop back to their master". A writer, too, who is a master of exact distinction. Jean de Meun, we see, "had not, like Dante, conquered", but "he had at least journeyed round the whole world of ideas and social life and character". So Jean de Meun must have "for his immediate followers, the practical utility of a general store, and for us he retains some of its chaotic attraction". Lewis's is a critical light which searches out the lesser as well as the greater names. There is this, for example, to be said of Thomas Usk: "His interweaving of divine and human love, if sometimes confusing, has an original turn . . . and in his style, while the faults are largely those of the models, the merits are his own." For even less promising objects of attention, the glance is lively and the expression spirited: "In Montgomerie we seem to hear the scrape of the fiddle and the beat of dancing on the turf."

So it is as the work of a writer, before all else, that *The Allegory of Love* continues to hold interest. Its schematism, as I have earlier suggested, is certainly over-rigid. "Courtly Love" is given its four distinguishing marks: Humility, Courtesy, Adultery, and the Religion of Love. There is a suspicious clarity, a hardness of outline, in this. Like an over-scrupulous examiner, or a vigilant border-guard, Lewis makes his firm allocations—so that Chaucer in his *Troilus and Criseyde* is seen as approaching "the very frontiers . . . of the romance of marriage": but Chaucer "does not himself cross the frontier". And of course there is always the feeling that Dorigen and Arveragus, in *The Franklin's Tale*, ought not really to have been married if the analysis is to hold good. Lurking in the background is that wariness of the present age and its regrettable tendencies which, enshrined in the dedication to Owen Barfield and made explicit in the preface, for the most part lies low in the chapters that follow, though it has its moments—as when D. H. Lawrence "writhes"; or Chaucer's *Troilus* is seen to be "modern" "because it is successfully and perfectly medieval"; or, again, in the gnomic observation that the best use of what is seen as "dated" is to ask ourselves what will most quickly date in the literature now in favour. Such questions were to come to the fore with increasing intensity in later works where Lewis established himself as the redoubtable controversialist of his day. *The Allegory of Love* remains compulsively readable, as few other works of historical literary criticism can claim to be, even in isolated passages; and if anyone can be said to have ended a tradition of dullness in scholarly writing, it is surely Lewis in this great, forever readable book.

I will say no more about "The Personal Heresy" (elaborated in the controversy with E. M. W. Tillyard). The prime ground of reservation is, the interest, surely justifiable in the *data* of quotidian existence—the poet as citizen, lover, taxpayer, friend, even the poet as critic of his own art—and the interaction between these and what emerges or is released in the work of art. We have learned to trust the tale, never the teller; but we cannot forbear to be interested in the teller *as* teller. Lewis shuts this completely out of sight, in a manner which suggests once more Barfield's sense of a power of willed exclusion which "became at length . . . an ingrained and effortless habit of soul". It is to my mind paradoxical that *A Preface to Paradise Lost* (1942) should enthusiastically contend for what on Lewis's own showing lies outside the scope of evaluative criticism—the presumed intentions and working purposes of an author. But I commend both the Personal Heresy controversy and the *Preface to Paradise Lost* as exhibiting in the highest degree the true skills of controversy, the expression of settled views with an uncompromising force of argument. Lewis is here most notably, as John Wain once called him, the pure advocate. His entrenched conservatism reminds me once more of his own genial choice of role in any "educational war"—the last ditch.

So the opening round of *A Preface to Paradise Lost* is gruffly argumentative: corkscrews and cathedrals are to be sharply distinguished. At the climax, it is a matter of "each to his own taste"; Satan's predicament could almost be seen to be "roaring farce"; and so on. But amidst these aggressive, thrusting passes at the reader there is to be found the most remarkable single piece of criticism in Lewis's entire output—the brilliant account of Vergil as one who "added a new dimension to poetry". Who can forget the characterisation of Aeneas as "a ghost of Troy until he becomes the father of Rome", or the masterly treatment of Vergil's sense of vocation "in the double character of a duty and a desire"? Lewis is at his best when controversy is laid aside and he comes to expound that which is central to the civilisation he honours. It is a vocation and in it duty and desire are inseparable. He did not, perhaps, exercise it often enough. The passage, from *The Allegory of Love*, in praise of Martianus Capella is one notable example: "The philosophies of others, the religions of others—back even to the twilight of pre-republican Rome—have all gone to the curiosity shop of his mind. It is not his business to believe or disbelieve them; the wicked old pedant knows a trick worth two of that. He piles them all up round him till there is hardly room for him to sit among them in the middle darkness of the shop; and there he gloats and catalogues, but never dusts them, for even their dust is precious in his eyes!" There both duty and desire find the happiest of meetings. It is so, again, when Lewis must face the fact—unwelcome to his narrative, and therefore needing to be honestly set down—that the fully-fledged allegorical poem when it at last emerges in the *Psychomachia* of Prudentius is "unworthy of the great utterances which lead up to it". Seneca, "with his imagery of life as a journey", it has to be said, was nearer the mark, for "The journey has its ups and downs, its pleasant resting-places enjoyed for a night and then abandoned, its unexpected meetings, its rumours of dangers ahead, and, above all, the sense of its goal, at first far distant and dimly heard of, but growing nearer at every turn of the road".

Is it possible that these passages speak to us more feelingly because of Lewis's own voluntary withdrawal from the things that pass away? The eagles and the trumpets appealed to him deeply: on him, no less than other moralists, Christian and pagan alike, "the discipline and circumstance of the legions" had made a lasting impression. But withdrawal made for no lack of warmth—a geniality which remarkably coexists with the cut and thrust of dialectic. His deepest regard is for that process of change which, giving place, in his view, to a greater goodness does not cancel, much less vilify, that which it has superseded; and so the old gods can be honoured: "the decline of the gods from deity to hypostasis and from hypostasis to decoration, was not, for them nor for us, a history of sheer loss. For decoration may let romance in. The poet is free to invent, beyond the limits of the possible, regions of strangeness and beauty for their own sake . . . I mean the 'other world' not of religion, but of imagination; the land of longing, the Earthly Paradise, the garden east of the sun and west of the moon". For Lewis, as the title-page of his *Pilgrim's Regress* had made clear, there was no quarrel with romanticism, properly understood, as there was none with reason; both were at one with Christianity. It is, as I have earlier argued, a striking synthesis. Its effect on Lewis, it must be allowed, was to discourage close curiosity about history, the grain and joint of past periods understood as such, much as it led to indifference about the characteristics of individual personalities. The invitation to contribute to the *Oxford History of English Literature* was prompted by his old tutor, F. P. Wilson, at a time when perhaps neither he nor Lewis had a clear sense that the connective work of historical survey within the limits of an assigned period was not in any sense Lewis's *forte*. However, Lewis laboured doggedly at it (OHEL pronounced "Oh, Hell" was his cheerful acronym for this self-imposed task), until the final proofreading in 1953.

In this book Lewis, as might be expected, is at his best in the accounts he gives of favourite authors—Dunbar, Sidney and, of course, Spenser, to take but three. But there is something uncomfortably constrained which derives, without doubt, from the plan of the series. Lewis has no bent for detecting order or pattern within set chronological limits. The exhilarating sweep of *The Allegory of Love* is not possible within the confines of a century, and his honesty of purpose forbids any stirring climax. "The historian," he had written some twenty years before the sixteenth-century treatment was to appear, "is not at liberty to dispose his fable as he would wish." So the close of the survey is in low key, almost flatly dispirited: "I do not suppose that the sixteenth century differs . . . from any other arbitrarily selected stretch of years. It illustrates well enough the usual complex, unpatterned historical process; in which, while men often throw away irreplaceable wealth, they not infrequently escape what seemed inevitable dangers, not knowing that they have done either nor how they did it."

Lewis's treatment is not made easier by certain obduracies. The reader will perhaps not be much hindered by the insistence on "Scotch" where he might expect "Scots" or "Scot-

tish" ("the freedom of 'my ain vulgair'"). But the stubbornness of "Papists" will bring some up short. It is all very well
to assert that the word "Papist" "is not now used dyslogistically
except in Ulster, and it is certainly not so intended here." But
this has the air of a false *naïveté*. Who can undo the harm of
dyslogistic usage? Lewis's own title-page quotation in *The
Allegory of Love* had been from the *Ars poetica* where Horace
asserts the over-riding force of what has become established
by usage. Let us continue the quotation. *Multa renascentur—*

> *vocabula, si volet usus,*
> *Quem penes arbitrium est et ius et norma loquendi.*

("Many a term now fallen from use shall have a second birth,
if usage will have it so—in whose hands is the arbitrament,
the right and the rule of speech.") There is an equal and opposite stubbornness in Lewis's use of the word "drab". He
intends to be merely descriptive. But how should he expect
his readers to cleanse the word of its associations of "unin-
spired", "dull", "pedestrian," and substitute "earnest", "heavy-
handed", "commonplace"? To be sure, common sense wins
when Lewis concedes that the word "reformation", while it
"begs the question", "is now so deeply entrenched in historical usage that I shall continue to employ it". It is some matter for relief: we would otherwise be in danger of having no
book at all. What is worse, because it is stubbornly inherent
in the whole treatment of the sixteenth century, is the refusal
of the concept, in any meaningful terms, of a "Renaissance".
One is reminded of Coghill's agreeable anecdote. Lewis, encountered in Addison's Walk, was indeed "pleased with himself": "'I believe', he answered with a modest smile of triumph,
'I *believe* I have proved that the Renaissance never happened
in England. *Alternatively*'—he held up his hand to prevent

my astonished exclamation—'that if it did, *it had no importance!'*" So the introductory chapter of *English Literature in
the Sixteenth Century* is firmly headed "New Learning and New
Ignorance"; and one can only say that the spirit of Old Knock
is rigorously at work. There is even, at times, the very tone
of that voice which had first put down the schoolboy who,
speaking innocently of "these fiendish German atrocities", was
reduced to "these brutal atrocities"—only to meet the steely
edge of the final rebuttal, "Is it not plain that we must call them
simply *Human*?" So, here: "Once we cease to let the humanists' own language beg the question, is it not clear that in this
context the 'barbarous' is the living and the 'classical' the still-
born?"

As we have seen, we can be thankful for Lewis's wary sense
that the modern reader, Latinless or virtually so, is not to be
delivered helpless into the hands of one party. Even so, virtuosity sometimes overreaches itself. Lewis had described his
always spirited renderings as undertaken "not simply for the
fun of it". There was, I am quite sure, a lot of "fun" for him
in the doing—a refreshment for an overall labour which became increasingly less attractive to him. I suspect the deepest reason for Lewis's inaptness for "history" in any sense
appropriate to the modern mind was his own relish for History as one of the great kinds—an order of exalted composi-
tion that searched out the exemplary and delighted in
proclaiming it. Short of this—and it was emphatically something not to be smuggled in—the honest writer's task (a "drab"
task, perhaps) was to report faithfully *ad hoc*.

What saves the book is Lewis's gift of phrase, aptly laconic
on almost every page. Thus he will concede to humanism one
veritable triumph—the victory over "gentlemanly philistinism"

which "slowly but surely decayed and was not reinstated till compulsory games altered the whole character of school life". There is a hobby-horse indeed. He brings it to life with the mock-judicial gravity of "There was thus a long lucid interval between Squire Western and Bertie Wooster". But drollery takes over: Lewis adds, and I am sure it is not entirely flippant, "it is arguable that during that interval England was at her greatest". We should hesitate to call this tongue-in-cheek; unless we allow for an Irish tongue, and, certainly, for Irish cheek. This sprightliness illuminates some very remote corners. Of *Bacchus' Bounty*, for example, it can be said that "The Bacchanalian spirit is well evoked but wearies us before the end". But this is not the last word before the work is returned to obscurity: "It is, however, a good book for a man to enrich his vocabulary: here are the 'coppernosed crue, the knuckledebunions of Rome' and 'that old Huddle and Twang, Aristodemus'." Equally, the well-known names of the period are safeguarded from languid misconception. "The mellow gold of the *Polity*", we are warned, "is not merely the natural overflow of a mild eupeptic who has good reason to be pleased with the *status quo*." Sometimes one catches the hint of a dutiful weariness: as here, setting out a sort of prolegomena to the *Polity*, Lewis first characterises the "ruthless antithesis" of puritanism (the "Barthianism" of its day), in setting "a God of inscrutable will 'over against' the 'accursed nature of Man' with all its arts, sciences, traditions, learning and merely human virtues". This is clear enough. But when we turn the page we are told that we must not expect definitive answers if we persist in asking Hooker what things are divine and what things "merely human": for "The word *merely* conceals precisely the point of view which Hooker declines". In other words, "merely" (we remember the potential ambiguity of *Mere Christianity*) may serve its turn for the prolegomena but is to be discarded when we come to grips with the work itself?

Some will by now suppose that I have come to bury Lewis not to praise him. Not so. There is no trace in him of the infirmities he diagnoses in "the old Chapman"—"digressive, cryptic, anxious to be wiser than nature allowed him". On the contrary, Lewis is alive and unfailingly alert in the penetralia of the sixteenth century, dealing patiently but briskly, for the most part equably, and striving to illuminate where he cannot unreservedly commend. Very like, in fact, his own Martianus Capella, with this difference that while assuredly, "there is hardly room" for anyone "to sit among" a vast accumulation of old books, Lewis's achievement is to press on, listing steadily, with an unerring gift for telling characterisation and, what is rarer among historians a scrupulousness of attention to even the least promising of works. He will even plead for a "reconsideration" of du Bartas as "long overdue"—the quaintest of pleas for perhaps as unlikely a candidate for rehabilitation as could readily be imagined.

The collection of essays entitled *Rehabilitations* appeared in 1939. It was the second of Lewis's books in the scholarly field: but it is characteristic of him that the collection includes several polemic pieces—two on the academic study of English—along with an exposition and a sample of alliterative verse, and an ingenious piece "Bluspels and Flalansferes" (subtitled "A semantic nightmare") which showed how readily Lewis could have taken his place among the "Clevers" of *Pilgrim's Regress*. His concern for right values in what may loosely be called Education is steadily apparent throughout his career. Whether it is the "social philosophy" of *The Abolition of Man* (1943), which starts with the values implicit in certain modes

of teaching English, or the excellent brevity and lucid exposition of *Studies in Words* (1960), the basis from which Lewis
argues is his own experience as tutor and lecturer. *Studies in
Words* sets out to demonstrate that "intelligence and sensibility by themselves are not enough". "Knowledge is necessary":
but this knowledge is imparted with a hunter's skill, and so
with an infectious, vivid enthusiasm—"the smallest semantic discomfort" should rouse our "suspicions". Above all, the
study offers something heartening for an age when "the lin-
guistic analysts have made us afraid that our thought may be
almost wholly conditioned by our speech". Lewis, by "driving words from different languages abreast", can feel he has
shown that "there is something, either in the structure of the
mind or in the things it thinks about, which can produce the
same results under very different conditions". Only a mind
as well furnished as Lewis's could in fact "drive abreast" in this
manner. The observations are telling, ranging beyond the
seminar-room. Verbicide, for example, is often committed by
men who "want to snatch a word as a party banner, to appropriate its 'selling quality'". There is a very human sagacity in
noting that "most people are obviously far more anxious to
express their approval and disapproval of things than to describe them". And the humour is gently effective in the genial parody:

> *Let no one say, and say it to your shame,*
> *That there was meaning here before you came.*

This book seems to me quite perfect. Who but Lewis could
interest the Greekless reader in *eleutheros*, and, in two pages,
make him wholly conversant with its main shades of meaning? Or call to muster in one company Augustine's Monica
taunted by her tippling slave; Figaro; Mrs. Slipslop; Sam Weller

(with his "diamond-cut-diamond" realism); and Philoctetes addressing the cunning Odysseus?—and all this in barely fifteen lines, carried off with breath-taking ease, so that the reader longs for more. Lewis's sheer erudition—the secure possession of acutely observed moments of pure enjoyment in an unequalled range of reading—captivates and exhilarates even at the seventieth times seven of re-reading. This is indeed to make the reader free; and once again the chief instrument of that freedom is Lewis's gift of apt and vivid translation. To take but one example of many: "The braggart in Phaedrus (v.ii) assures his fellow traveller that he will pursue the man who has robbed them both and 'see that he learns' (*curabo sentiat*) what sort of people he has meddled with. The English would be 'I'll show him'." It is all there: accuracy, ease, and pointed application. "I'll larn him", we may add—with gratitude and affection—might well stand as Lewis's permanent slogan. In this little work lies the thesaurus of a life-time's reading, guarded by an arsenal of sardonic observation: as, "It would have been far more wounding to be called *swine* when the word still carried some whiff of the sty and some echo of a grunt; far more wounding to be called a *villain* when this still conjured up an image of the unwashed, malodorous, gross, belching, close-fisted and surly boor". But now?—"Now, who cares? Language meant solely to hurt hurts strangely little."

I see *An Experiment in Criticism* (1961) as similarly issuing from the same fullness of experience as teacher and reader, but this time with a polemical energy that perhaps will convert few while it cannot fail to absorb at every turn. There is the same deft skill in analogy. For example, the manifest danger in going to an author "chiefly to find further confirmation for our belief that it teaches this or that, rather than for a fresh immersion in what it is". True, but forever unforgettable when we are told that, doing this, "We shall be like a man poking his fire, not to boil the kettle or warm the room, but in the hope of seeing in it the same pictures he saw yesterday". That can only be called brilliant.

The climax of the book is, of course, the attack upon the Vigilant school of criticism, the "watchdogs or detectives" whose acerbity may perhaps be excused (for "A sincere inquisitor or a sincere witch-finder can hardly do his chosen work with mildness"); but who nevertheless are to be held in large measure responsible for the present state of higher study, with its "Young people drenched, dizzied, and bedevilled by criticism to a point at which primary literary experience is no longer possible". A state of affairs, indeed, which constitutes "a far greater threat to our culture than any of those from which the Vigilants would protect us".

This is well said, and the whole little book will be valued most by those who have most cause to lament the virtual disappearance of the "all-important conjunction (Reader Meets Text)". But the paradoxical leap which Lewis makes, to fix "attention on the act of reading", is to invite us to consider as good that literature which "permits, invites, or even compels, good reading; and bad, as that which does the same for bad reading". It is a leap which dazzles—and perhaps in its own way darkens—counsel. Isn't there, one wonders, something to be said (qualitatively) about the reader who is in touch with his own age and the one who, wilfully or all unawares, is out of touch? If we are to value criticism at all, it must be, at the very highest when the impulse that moves the reader to turn critic, to speak to his fellow-men of what he has encountered in the work, approaches the same order of intensity that moved the writer. *C'est plus fort que moi* is the one impulse that must drive writer and reader alike—the one to create and the other to respond. What will not serve is a willed exclusion by writer or reader from a continuing present of literary and critical activity. Here, too, a Lewisian maxim holds, *Nobis quoque militandum*: "We, too, have a fight on our hands." I place *An Experiment in Criticism* among Lewis's late, golden works—a repository of delighted learning and a quieter temper of controversial skill. No one, of whatever party, could read it without sheer admiration. I do not know that there have been many conversions; and the reason is not far to seek. No one ever spoke from so full and unjaded an experience as reader. Wasn't it only a fortnight before he died that he took up *Les liaisons dangéreuses*? And his comment?: "Wow, what a book!" All beyond emulation.

With *The Discarded Image* (1964) we return to what Lewis does best—an unrivalled power of wide-ranging exposition in brief space, drawing effortlessly upon direct acquaintance with each text cited, and condensing with entire fidelity ideas of vast range and, hitherto, puzzling indeterminacy. It certainly fulfils the author's hope of a kind of scholarly undertaking that would not be "always taking you *out of* the literature itself". We remember the aversion, at the outset of Lewis's first extended work of scholarship, *The Allegory of Love*, from "that itch for 'revival', that refusal to leave any corpse ungalvanised, which is among the more distressing accidents of scholarship". Here, one of his last books, we have an instance of scholarship which, truly, "leads *in*". It is, too, an instance of what might properly be called a "background" book, a genuine history of ideas. All too often—indeed, it almost seems an invariable happening—the reader of such works is confronted with a *résumé* of the principal thinkers of a period set beside the implied thought-patterns of the poets, dramatists, and novelists. But the real (and harder) business of exposition should be to disentangle the plain misunderstandings, the veritable misapprehensions, which may be the real soil for creative imagination. Lewis is the first to point out that the dominant pattern of an age in genuinely literary terms is an abstraction from any "total Model": "It takes over . . . only what is intelligible to a layman and only what makes some appeal to imagination and emotion. Thus our own backcloth contains plenty of Freud and little of Einstein."

I have good cause to remember this, for I once mentioned the possibilities of a book conceived not as a history of thought but as an account of the differences between the declared positions of thinkers in any given age and the misunderstandings, the potentially fertile misconceptions, of their literary contemporaries. "There is only one drawback", he murmured. "By a process familiar to all of us your book will come to be known as *Lawlor's Misunderstandings*." I can only hope that these present observations of mine will not wholly deserve that characterisation.

To sum up: I have suggested that Tillyard's enthusiastic commendation of Lewis when *The Allegory of Love* first appeared—"At last . . . a medievalist who is also a critic"—has the terms of praise the wrong way round. There was cause for rejoicing in the arrival of a critical writer who was also a medievalist. So I have called my brief treatment "The Writer as Scholar". It is the achieved directness of the writing that repeatedly astonishes. Try, for comparison, almost any discursive scholarly writer—say, on the theme of love in literature, Martin D'Arcy's *The Mind and Heart of Love* (1945). D'Arcy's is a book to be mentioned with honour—learned, original, enthusiastic, full of the real life of discursive intelligence. Let me say simply that it is absolutely complementary to Lewis's own extended writing. With D'Arcy you are lost in a beguiling labyrinth: *ambages pulcerrime* are the stock-in-trade of that beautiful mind. But with Lewis your feet are everywhere on the ground; the skyline is always in view. Ironic and paradoxical Lewis may be: but his is an incomparably solid achievement as the firm exponent of matters of real complexity and, sometimes, of an almost evanescent abstraction. The mere snobbery of "modernity" was a persistent challenge. (Though it weakened towards the end: "My finger grows weary of hornet's nests", he wrote to me from Cambridge.) But what he had said in the preface to *The Allegory of Love*, in dedicating the book to his friend Owen Barfield ("wisest and best" of his "unofficial teachers") records a major debt. He had been taught "not to patronize the past, and . . . to see the present as itself a 'period'". There is of course a limitation in this: for him all periods were equal, but some were more equal than others. Yet when he spoke out against the present it was against what he took to be not presuppositions but manifest errors. His constant state, as tutor and scholar, is best described in what he wrote of himself on receiving Tillyard's rejoinder to his original foray on "The Personal Heresy". He was a man "hungry for rational opposition".

While, undoubtedly, all his work is of a piece, two of his narratives throw particular light on his interests in literary study. I have spoken rather slightingly of the *Preface to Paradise Lost* for what it has to say about Milton. But what it tells us of Lewis's own exalted imagination is finely complemented in *Perelandra*, where once again a Fall, it seems, is to be re-enacted; but this time there is a happy turn—a *eucatastrophe*, to use that admirable coinage of Tolkien's. There is one other piece of narrative to be mentioned, and I would place it above all others. *Till We Have Faces* is truly a "myth" in the sense

which Lewis himself defined in his *Experiment in Criticism*—
a story which "depends hardly at all on such usual narrative
attractions as suspense or surprise" and communicates the
sense of that which is "not only grave but awe-inspiring". For
once, Lewis attained something which he approved above all
else and for which (in his earliest article) he had revered *Comus*,
a "dearly bought singleness of quality"—

> *smooth and full as if one gush*
> *Of life had washed it.*

To say so much is of course very far from suggesting that
the other writings are not worth close attention. I can claim
to have read most of what Lewis published, and I find myself
re-reading a good deal of the narrative fiction. Had anyone
before C. P. Snow described a College meeting more vividly
than Lewis in *That Hideous Strength*? How well one knows
"the Progressive Element", including its puppet-leader Curry,
a sub-Warden "so used to superintending the lives of his colleagues that it came naturally to him to superintend their
deaths".

One phrase will serve—that "quiet fullness of ordinary nature" which Lewis honoured in George Macdonald. The words
stand at the head of the final chapter of *The Allegory of Love*.
In Lewis's own life a "quiet fullness" meant that the transcendental was never at variance with the prosaic. When "Joy"
came, while it "made all my erotic and magical perversions
of Joy look like sordid trumpery, it had no such disenchant-
ing power over the bread upon the table or the coals in the
grate". There was no split in Lewis's personality between the
strong sense of fact and the region of high imagination. The
"romantic theology" which Lewis shared with and in part

learned from Charles Williams gave to heightened awareness of the external world the decisive role in man's understanding of his complex nature.

It is as certain as these things can be that we shall not see another like him—at least, in making the same intellectual voyage. The record he gave in *Pilgrim's Regress* was, as he later wryly admitted, based upon incomprehension of the modern mind. "I committed the same sort of blunder as one who should narrate his travels through the Gobi Desert on the assumption that this route was as familiar to the British public as the line from Euston to Crewe." But if his work in English studies is to be advanced, two starting-points offer themselves for re-investigation—medieval *fyne amour*, and rebellious romanticism. Each was in some measure an opponent of, and each became in some degree a successful usurper on, the fullness of religious experience. *Fyne amour* stands over against religion apprehended primarily as morality, emergent romanticism challenges religion as the revelation of final reality.

I sometimes imagine a single book that would synthesize Lewis's life-work as an English scholar. It might begin with eighteenth-century antiquarian interest in the medieval past, and by comparing the imagined "Gothick" era with the real Middle Ages it would recover some of the ground lost to abstraction and simplification in that first scholarly debate. It would then survey poetical appropriation of this imagined past, from Romanticism full blown up to the death of romantic individualism in the middle and later nineteenth century. The course of the argument, so far, would be to show, first, the identification of heightened experience with longing for a supposedly lost "world of fine fabling", piquant and arresting because unalterably removed from actuality; second, this bitter-sweet experience of longing becoming at the hands of major poets the touchstone of all significance, the evidence of "Imagination, awful Power". Now the setting and apparatus, all the beguiling legacy of "the fairy way of writing", offers itself to the poet as the perfect medium for what is otherwise inexpressible. Precisely because every tincture of belief in its objective existence has gone. "A frightful fiend" can be the fitting embodiment of nameless dread only when no fiend is to be met in waking reality. This part of the book would amply demonstrate Lewis's own recognition that the old gods had to die before "they could wake again in the beauty of acknowledged myth". The myth, in turn, must fly at the touch of a colder religion.

The third part of our investigation might point forward past this death to another re-awakening, this time in the present century, when T. S. Eliot, the former opponent of romanticism (and on that score one of Lewis's earlier targets) comes to celebrate a Christianity that ascends from penitential sadness to a final certainty, when reason and imagination are no longer at variance:

> *And all shall be well and*
> *All manner of thing shall be well*
> *When the tongues of flame are in-folded*
> *Into the crowned knot of fire*
> *And the fire and the rose are one.*

It is of course a book that would run counter to many established half-truths and as such have to contest every inch of the way. But then—to quote one of Lewis's supreme poets—it always was so:

> *Sed revocare gradum superasque evadere ad auras,*
> *Hic opus, hic labor est.*

Lewis's central gift, so deep-rooted it is apparent from the first of his scholarly writings and flourishes unabated in the last, is his grasp of what may be called the intellectual imagination. "Unity and vastness", as in *Piers Plowman*, he wrote, may have been attained, "by thought rather than by sense, but they end by being a true image and no mere conception". If this is the true poetic power, we may learn from Lewis that the true critical power is complementary to it. The poet's capacity at its highest is to render "imaginable what before was only intelligible". The reader, in his turn, can wholeheartedly respond: for nothing less is on offer than an enlargement of our sense of the intelligible. There, I believe is the lasting debt of historical literary criticism to a writer who had himself practised as poet and philosopher—a philosopher on whom, in a very special sense, "cheerfulness kept breaking in", that news from a far country which sustained and illuminated his pilgrimage.

Perhaps this achievement—more nearly a "unified sensibility" than anything we have seen in recent times—was possible only to a poet who had in his own estimation failed, and to a philosopher who had been left behind when the great dynasty of the Idealists had taken as mighty a fall as Ozymandias. Perhaps so: but, then, as Lewis had long come to realise, his religion was a school in which good use can be made of whatever talents the entrant might bring with him. Lewis's greatest gifts are those of a truly authoritative guide. In matters literary as well as theological and spiritual, he tells you nothing that he has not himself long since known at first hand; he takes you nowhere he himself has not tested for soundness of footing. A guide, then, with an experienced guide's capacity, on occasion, for a certain impatience and a certain jovial indifference to any neophyte cavilling. What would you not give, he once wrote, offering himself as a guide to Milton, to have a real live Epicurean at your side when you are reading Lucretius? What would not any of us give, wherever the road may turn, to have a real and abundantly live *reader* as our unfailing guide?

As a guide, then, quite incomparable. But perhaps Lewis is less to be thought of as a guide of the venerable Vergilian sort than as one who has cheerful kinship with the guides to be met in those medieval French vision-poems which especially delighted him. There, in the hiatus between falling asleep in the real world and the beginning of adventures in the world of vision, it was a Friendly Animal who came to the reader's aid. It is perhaps no coincidence that in a well-loved poem by Machaut the all-important guide is not other than a Lion. All Lewis's readers, whatever the aspect of a many-sided achievement that gives special delight, must experience a special gratitude and affection towards an author who, effortlessly and consistently, is a true embodiment of his own Aslan.

Postscript

IN PUTTING TOGETHER these recollections of Lewis, I have asked myself once again what, four-square and irrefutably, was absolutely distinctive—perhaps unique—in his make-up. I have to say that it was his being able to accept, with unusual simplicity and absolute constancy, the concept of Divine forgiveness of sin. Not, of course, in simply assenting to the doctrine; but in being unforcedly able to receive it, and to rejoice in it as objective fact, so that henceforward there could be no dwelling on failure. Newness of life sustained a special receptivity to each day's offering to the senses and imagination. The breach between reason, discursively understood, and heightened awareness of the external world—a chasm which had daunted and even devastated others—was simply transcended. And, most notably, there was to be no diminution in ratiocinative ardour, but, rather, an unflagging readiness to defend the faith that was in him.

It will mislead if this is thought of especially, or indeed perhaps at all, as a matter of the will. (One recalls Barfield's sense of something *voulu*, the presence, as it seemed, of "not one, but two Lewises".) Perhaps I can offer another perspective. For me, Lewis effortlessly overrides William James's all but incontrovertible allocation of religious experience between the tough-minded and the tender-minded. Not that there was any lack of sensibility ("alarmingly vulnerable" is Farrer's accurate observation), either emotionally or intellectually. Lewis more than once admitted to thinking of things that frightened him; and, equally, there were times when the whole system of Christian belief struck him as distinctly unlikely. But it remained simply beyond any question whatever that if you believed in the forgiveness of sin there was nothing to do but most thankfully to accept it. He once clarified this by reminding an anxious correspondent that when the sun stands overhead at noon, it casts no shadow of the man beneath.

Not, then, a matter of the will, simply understood. Rather, something to be seen in all its rarity as a special gift, a quality so uncommon as to be secure beyond envy because incapable of mere emulation—in Burke's noble phrase, an "unbought grace". Its ultimate occasion, to be sure, can be placed accurately in that re-reading of the *Hippolytus* which brought Lewis to obedience. There, he records, he "had simply been ordered—or, rather, compelled—to 'take that look off my face'." This, the First Move, was at once known as a move to last. There was to be no question of "returning to the desert": the look was never to be resumed. Equally, with the last transition to be made, there was to be an end of ambiguity in any terminology that we might seek to apply. Now the right question to put was "Freedom, or necessity? Or do they differ at their maximum?" And, as to Will, no less than Emotion, "we have a secret suspicion that the great passion or the iron resolution is partly a put-up job". So a false conception of adulthood came tumbling down, to release a perpetually youthful energy (Kathleen Raine's "boyish greatness") which could bemuse even close friends (one thinks of Barfield's astonished reaction at the joyous sally into "pure pastiche"). It is not, of course, to be seen in any account of the recollected path towards conversion. There the keynote is reluctance shading into pure dread (The Mouse's Search for the Cat). But it is manifest in the awareness of instant compliance—an unbuckling, loosening the rein, the snowman beginning to trickle. These are not activities of the will, subject to Farrer's just dictum, "What will has caused, will must be brought to correct". God moves in a mysterious way, even on buses going up Headington hill. Lewis records nothing more nor less than a mystery, inviolate for himself as for all others, an experienced and irrevocable surrender.

What is no mystery is the joyous turn to happiness, truly a *eucatastrophe*. In him it is a return, a regress (if we can, for the moment, clear the term of the dyslogistic overtones it has for modern ears). When conversion came it brought acceptance of "Mother Kirk"—a sturdy indifference to anything that might be at variance with the Ulster Protestantism of his boyhood (notwithstanding any private practices he himself might find helpful); and, above all, that solid and unyielding adherence to a "mere" Christianity which justly made him the most influential apologist of his day. Lewis's zeal to do battle against all comers was, by the happiest of paradoxes, based on the deepest awareness that his true calling was *not* to "propound" but rather to "live through" what, uniting all sides of his nature, he perceived as "a sort of ontological proof".

The contrast I have earlier made with Johnson may show, perhaps too painfully, that an overpowering sense of a Divine Lawgiver can make a desert of the heart. But what if, blessedly, for once a simple submission could be enacted?—the gift accepted in its entirety and the beneficiary going forward into an experienced new life with a lightness of heart never to be wholly subdued?

The two climactic events of Lewis's earlier life were the utterly devastating loss of his mother and the subsequent discovery of another mother's love in the household set up with Mrs. Moore. With Lewis's conversion he set himself steadfastly to an unremitting domestic obedience—that domestic slavery which even so close and affectionate an observer as Warnie found totally inexplicable. But surely it manifested a boy's determination to make amends? Plenty of scope for the will there; and, it is to be insisted, nothing at variance with the sense of high adventure —the realisation that man is called not simply to obedience, but to a daily experience of the created Universe in which he will have "tasted and seen" a Creator worthy of adoration.

High adventure? It is a quality which we in our day are not well placed to perceive, inheriting as we do that dread of the unconditional unforgettably expressed by Kierkegaard as a terror of "walking in the gloom". For Lewis's latter-day readers his "journey from Euston to Crewe" must be a journey from Copenhagen to Freiburg with animated exchanges in Paris. Kierkegaard and Heidegger, no less than Sartre and Camus, have brought us to prize as only authentic a truth to be known in moments of wholly indeterminate anxiety or plain dread. If we were to hope for a way forward it could only be in revelation conceived as, dare we say, a focused certainty. And to that the due response must be either lasting aversion or a dejected submission.

In his deepest trial of all, Lewis was granted a sense that "some shattering and disarming simplicity is the real answer". We should dwell on "disarming": the dialectician's task was never to be discredited; but it could be simply supplanted. It is perfectly characteristic of Lewis that this realisation came like "the sound of a chuckle in the darkness". We shall not be in range of Lewis's special gift if we are unable to grasp that, for once in modern religious experience, a superb quality of obedience was inseparable from a sense of unfathomable happiness.

Who but Lewis could write, not long before his death, submitting the genial proposal that it was Lazarus who should be honoured rather than Stephen as the true protomartyr? Being brought back from death *was*, he had to admit, "rather hard". But of course there was always the possibility that Prison visiting might be allowed, to solace those who would be, as he himself hoped to be, in Purgatory. What sanctioned this lightness of heart? Writing to a woman religious he could count on a profoundly shared awareness—"It *is* all rather fun—solemn fun—isn't it?"

Index

A Note on the Author

John Lawlor was C. S. Lewis's undergraduate pupil at Magdalen College, Oxford, graduating in 1939 with first class honors and remaining a close friend of Lewis's thereafter. After serving with the Devonshire Regiment in Italy during World War II, he pursued graduate studies under the supervision of J. R. R. Tolkien. He was a founding member, in 1950, of the International Association of University Professors of English and served as its Secretary General and Treasurer from 1971 to 1995. Now emeritus professor of English language and literature at the University of Keele in Great Britain, he has written widely on medieval and Renaissance English literature and on higher education. Professor Lawlor and his wife divide their time between homes in Cornwall and Tokyo.

This book was designed and set into type
by Mitchell S. Muncy,
with cover art by Stephen J. Ott,
and printed and bound
by Quebecor Printing Book Press
Brattleboro, Vermont.

The text face is Minion,
designed by Robert Slimbach
and issued in digital form by Adobe Systems,
Mountain View, California, in 1991.

The paper is acid-free and is of archival quality.

12